The Presidential Contest

The Presidential Contest

With a Guide to the 1980 Race

Richard A. Watson
University of Missouri—Columbia

John Wiley & Sons
New York   Chichester   Brisbane   Toronto

Library of Congress Cataloging in Publication Data:

Watson, Richard Abernethy, 1923–
    The presidential contest.

    Includes indexes.
    1.   Presidents—United States—Election.
I.   Title.
JK524.W38   329′.023′73092   79-17871
ISBN 0-471-05642-1

Printed in the United States of America
10 9 8 7 6 5 4 3 2 1

**To the Memory of
Hubert Horatio Humphrey**

Preface

I first began to follow presidential contests in 1948, the year Harry Truman bested Thomas Dewey in one of the biggest upsets in American political history. A quick comparison with 1976, when another vice president-became-president, Gerald Ford, fought unsuccessfully against Jimmy Carter to retain his office, reveals how these contests have changed over the years. Truman entered nine presidential primaries, winning easily in all of them; Ford battled the other major Republican contender, Ronald Reagan, in twenty-five primaries, winning in fifteen of them. Truman conducted a whistle-stop campaign, crisscrossing the nation by rail, and frequently speaking to voters in small towns late at night or very early in the morning; Ford challenged Carter to a series of three nationally televised debates and then conducted a media blitz in the last ten days of the campaign. At one point, two wealthy Oklahomans had to put up the money to get the Truman train back to Washington; the Ford campaign was supported by $25 million from a federal subsidy provided by American taxpayers. The political pollsters confidently pronounced Dewey as the victor weeks before the 1948 election (George Gallup questioned why the Republican committee would want to spend any more money when the election outcome was a foregone conclusion); in 1976 Gallup and his colleagues polled the American electorate right up to election eve, ultimately pronouncing the Ford-Carter race too close to call. Thus, although less than three decades separated the two presidential contests, in some respects they were political light-years apart.

Fortunately, increased attention to presidential contests has kept pace with rapid changes in the process by which we choose our chief executives. Since 1952, political scientists have studied presidential nominations closely, often under the auspices of the Brookings Institution and, more recently, the American Enterprise Institute. Also in 1952, an interdisciplinary team of political scientists, sociologists, and social psychologists at the University of Michigan began interviewing a nationwide sample of Americans on their voting behavior in the presidential contest, a project that has been repeated every election since that time. Nonacademic persons have also added to our understanding of presidential politics. Included are political pollsters such as Gallup, Harris, and Roper, who have provided information on voters' attitudes on candidates and issues; journalists such as Pulitzer prize-winning author Theodore White, who chronicled the 1960, 1964, 1968, and 1972 campaigns; and campaign managers, consultants, and advisers, many of whom gathered at the John Fitzgerald Kennedy School of Government at Harvard University to discuss the strategies and tactics of the 1972 and 1976 campaigns.

I have drawn from these and many other sources in writing this book. (Sources are identified in the text, and full information about them is contained in the references listed at the back of the book.) Its major purpose is to fit together the many aspects of the selection process so that the reader can view the presidential contest in its entirety. The material is presented in chronological order as the contest progresses so that persons can follow the process and see how each stage relates to the preceding one.

I had two major audiences in mind when I wrote this book. One consists of college students who are taking courses—including a beginning one in American government—that in some way cover the presidential contest. The other audience is much broader—journalists, politicians, or other persons in this country and abroad who are interested in a better understanding of the American presidential contest.

A brief introduction discusses the nature of democratic elections in general and the presidential election in particular. Chapter 1 begins with a short description of the evolution of the nomination process from its earliest beginning to the adoption of the national party conventions that both parties presently use to nominate their presidential candidates. Recent changes in the nomination rules (of which there have been many, especially for the Democrats), the reasons for such changes, and the effect these changes have had on presidential candidacies and contests are explained.

Having established this historical and legal background, Chapter 2 follows the dynamics of the nomination campaign from the candidates' early maneuvering for position through contesting in state primaries and caucus-conventions to the formal nomination by the national party convention. This information helps the reader to understand how candidates and their staffs view the campaign and the kinds of decisions they must make at successive stages of the contest. The chapter closes with an analysis of the increased participation by rank and file voters in recent presidential nominations.

The general election campaign is the subject of Chapter 3. I have found that the electoral college process is not an easy one for many students to grasp, but they understand it better if they appreciate the original thinking behind its establishment, how the nature of the college has changed over time, and how it presently shapes candidates' strategies and the outcome of the general election. The remainder of the chapter treats the dynamics of the general election campaign as candidates utilize various kinds of political appeals and choose the best means to communicate such appeals to the American voter.

Chapter 4, which deals with voting in presidential elections, first traces the progressive extension of the franchise to more and more Americans and then analyzes the extent to which persons have actually exercised their right to vote in recent elections. The rest of the chapter examines the effect that political party affiliation, social group and class identification, candidate appeal, issues, and events have on the voting decisions of the American people.

In these four chapters I have confined myself primarily to reporting and integrating what other persons have had to say about presidential contests. The final chapter is more in the form of an "editorial"; it offers my own reactions to such contests. It includes a personal assessment of what is right and wrong about the way we choose the chief executive and what we can and should do to make the process better.

Appendixes A, B, and C contain information designed to help the reader follow the upcoming campaign as it develops. Included are a schedule of the 1980 presidential primaries (Appendix A), profiles of the major candidates (Appendix B), and the rules of the 1980 contest and the 1976 results in each of the states (Appendix C).

I appreciate the assistance that I have received from many people in writing this book. Foremost have been the hundreds of students in my American presidency course over the last twenty years. Their high level of interest and probing questions have forced me to try to think through both the complicated rules that govern our presidential contests and the political factors that shape the strategies and results of such contests. Two of my colleagues, Michael Fitzgerald and David Leuthold, analyzed data for the section on voting in presidential elections. Elaine Kamarck and Penny Wydominic at the Democratic National Committee and Josephine Good and Emily Landis at the Republican National Committee provided me with information on the upcoming presidential contest that I used in the Appendixes. Wayne Anderson, my editor at Wiley, encouraged me at every stage of the project, as did my wife, Joan, who typed and helped edit the book.

Finally, I want to express my esteem for the late Senator Hubert Humphrey, to whom the book is dedicated. Although he had no direct involvement in it, he indirectly affected the book in countless ways. He graced American politics for some thirty years and was a major candidate in four presidential contests. When I think about these contests and of the qualities a presidential candidate should possess, I still think of him.

Columbia, Missouri
August 1979

Richard A. Watson

Contents

The Presidential Contest

Introduction

In a democratic society, elections constitute the major means by which those "outside" the government pass judgment on those "inside" the government. Periodically, major officeholders are required to come before the populace to have their right to exercise political power renewed. Also operating as part of the system is the availability of one or more alternative groups of leaders that voters can choose to govern them if they are dissatisfied with the performance of their present leaders. As Joseph Schumpeter (1950: 269) suggests, in a democracy individuals acquire the right to make political decisions by means of a "competitive struggle for the people's vote."*

The "competitive struggle for the people's vote" is a continuous process as leaders in and out of power attempt to convince the voters that they would fare better under their particular administration. However, the major effort to win over the electorate is concentrated during the period immediately preceding the election. During this time, candidates for office mount campaigns that involve a variety of political appeals designed to motivate the general public to take the time and effort to vote, and to vote for them.

According to democratic theory, political campaigns and elections perform a

*As discussed in Chapter 4, the concept of "people's vote" has changed over the years in the United States as the franchise has been extended to more and more groups; this trend toward broader public participation is also a feature of democratic elections.

variety of important functions in society. As Stephen Hess (1974: Chap. 4) suggests, they are primarily a process of "personnel selection," with the electorate operating as a "gigantic search committee" for the nation's political leaders. However, campaigns and elections also serve other purposes. As previously indicated, they offer a "corrective" for past electoral mistakes, the chance to "throw the rascals out," and to give a new team a chance to govern the nation. Campaigns also enable candidates to identify the major problems faced by a society and to propose policies and programs for dealing with such problems; viewed in this way, campaigns are "educational," a basic civics lesson for the electorate. The electoral process can also be a catharsis, enabling societal conflicts to be made public and thereby better faced. Such a process may also lead to another function of democratic elections: developing attitudes of political compromise and furthering social consensus (Janowitz and Marvick, 1956: 2).

Although elections of major public officials are important in any democratic society, they are especially so in the United States because of our presidential form of government. Under the parliamentary system used in most of the other democracies in the world, the voters do not directly choose the nation's executive officials; instead they choose the members of the legislative body, who bargain with each other over the composition of the cabinet, including its leader, usually called the prime minister. But in the United States, the presidential election is separate from legislative contests, so that voters pass judgment directly on the candidates for the nation's highest office. In addition, the fact that we have a two-party rather than a multiparty system also means that most of the votes tend to go to the two major candidates, with the winner generally receiving a significant percentage of the total popular vote.*

Another distinguishing feature of American presidential contests is the major role that the voters play in the *nomination* of candidates for the nation's highest office. In most other democratic societies, political party leaders, acting through committees or conferences, choose persons to represent them in the general election. In the United States the two major parties use national conventions comprised of delegates chosen from all the states to select their candidates. However, as indicated in Chapter 1, in recent years the choice of these delegates has been vested more and more in rank-and-file voters instead of merely in people who have traditionally been active in party affairs. As a result, the nomination, as well as the election of the president, has become a contest in which candidates must establish their popularity with the average voter.

These reasons—along with the important powers of the office—make the

---

*The winning presidential candidate must receive a majority of the votes in the electoral college (see Chapter 3). Since the Civil War, the electoral-college winner has never failed to receive at least 40 percent of the popular vote and has usually received more than 50 percent of that vote.

contest for the American presidency the most significant democratic election in the world. In no other country do so many voters cast their ballot directly for a single officeholder. Nowhere else does a single political campaign last as long and involve as many people or the expenditure of so much money. No other electoral contest receives as much coverage from the mass media. By any standard, an American presidential contest is the "World Series" of electoral politics.

CHAPTER 1

The Rules of the Nomination Contest

Individuals who seek the presidency today must pass through a long and complicated process by which Americans test aspirants for the nation's highest office. Moreover, they must survive two separate tests of political strength. First, candidates must win their party's nomination for the presidency; then, they must emerge victorious in the general election over the major party rival.

What makes the process particularly difficult for candidates is the fact that the nomination and election phases are so different. The rules for the two contests are distinctive. Campaign strategies and techniques must be especially tailored for the two stages of the presidential battle. Also, the participants in the two contests are different: those who help choose presidential nominees have been labeled by Hugh Heclo (1973: 25) as the "selectorate," as contrasted to the "electorate," which casts its vote in the general election.

The characteristic nomination and election phases of the presidential contest have developed over the course of American political history. The Founders never contemplated this separation in the procedure they devised for choosing our chief executive. However, as outlined in this chapter, major developments in the young nation soon resulted in the division of the selection process into two component parts. Moreover, as we will see, after the process became divided, changes continued to occur in both the nomination and election of the president.

THE EVOLUTION OF THE NOMINATION PROCESS

During the nation's first seven years, there was no separate procedure for nominating the president. The system operated as the Founders intended: members of the political elite from the various states, acting through the mechanism of the electoral college (see Chapter 4), chose George Washington to lead the country in 1789 and again in 1792. Persons with different political views agreed that the nation's wartime hero was a "patriot king" who would rule in the interests of all the people.

In Congress, however, no such political consensus prevailed. In 1790 Alexander Hamilton, the first secretary of the treasury in the Washington administration, presented an economic program that provided, among other matters, for the creation of a national bank and the passage of a tariff to protect American manufacturers and merchants from foreign competition. Thomas Jefferson (who was then serving as secretary of state) and James Madison (who sat in Congress) opposed such measures as benefiting only mercantile interests and not the nation's farmers, for whom they had great admiration. Subsequently, Jefferson and Madison also split with Hamilton on the Jay Treaty, which was negotiated with England in 1793 by the Washington administration. Under its terms the British agreed to withdraw troops from forts in the Northwest. However, the treaty failed to satisfy two other basic grievances that concerned Jefferson and Madison: one was compensation for slaves carried away during the Revolutionary War; the other was impressment into the British Navy of American sailors who served on American ships that were seized by the British for trading with the French (with whom the English were at war).

An important institution not provided for by the American Constitution—a system of political parties—emerged out of these controversies over domestic and foreign policy. The *Federalists,* with Hamilton acting as the major initiator of policies and Washington as the popular leader around whom men could be rallied, had formed by the early 1790s. They soon had candidates running for Congress as Federalists and voting in the legislature in favor of the Hamiltonian programs (Chambers, 1963: Chap. 2). Jefferson's resignation from the Washington administration in 1793 and Madison's opposition to Hamilton's programs in Congress paved the way for the formation of a rival political party, the *Republicans.** By the middle of the decade, cohesive pro- and antiadministration blocs were voting against each other in Congress (Charles, 1956: 93–94); soon congressional candidates were being identified with the Republicans as well as with the Federalists. The retirement of the popular George Washington at the end of his second term in 1796 created the potential for the spread of party politics from Congress to the presidency.

The development of political parties in the United States thus ended the brief system of the president's selection by the political elite of the day and injected the

---

*The party was sometimes called the "Democratic-Republicans" and later became the Democratic party.

choice of the nation's chief executive into the battleground of party politics. This development also required the parties to devise some means of choosing candidates to run under their party name, a process known as *nomination*. In 1796 the Federalists used consultation among their prominent leaders to choose their candidate, John Adams. The Republicans turned to their party members in Congress to nominate Thomas Jefferson as their standard-bearer. Four years later the Federalists followed suit, and the congressional caucus became the nominating mechanism for both parties.

The Congressional Caucus

The use of the congressional caucus made a lot of sense in this early stage of party development. Transportation problems were avoided because congressmen were already assembled in the nation's capital; moreover, since they were few in number, their task of nominating was manageable. Congressmen were also quite knowledgeable about potential presidential candidates from all parts of the new country. Thus, members of the "party-in-the-government" (those who held public office) were logical agents to choose candidates for the presidency with its nationwide constituency.

However, the congressional caucus also had some serious defects. It violated the separation-of-powers principle of the Constitution to have members of the legislative body play a key role in determining who would be president. The caucus also failed to represent areas in which the party lost the previous congressional election. In addition, interested and informed citizens who participated in party activities at the grass-roots level (especially in campaigns) took no part in the deliberations of the congressional caucus.

In time these defects began to undermine the congressional caucus system. The Federalists were the first to be affected. As their political fortunes waned, the size of the party's congressional delegation declined so much that it was no longer a viable and representative body. The party was forced to turn to alternative nominating devices. In 1808 and again in 1812, the Federalists gathered in what Gerald Pomper (1966: 17) calls "primitive national conventions": meetings of state delegates closed to people not specifically invited (only about one-half the states were represented) and also to the general public. In 1816, in the last presidential election contested by the Federalists (the party lost public support as a result of internal divisions, failure to organize at the grass-roots level, and the pro-British attitude of many of its leaders during the War of 1812), Rufus King was named as the party nominee without any formal party action.

The Republicans had a quite different experience with the congressional caucus. The party used it between 1800 and 1820 to nominate and to elect successfully a series of Virginians who had previously served as secretary of state—Thomas Jefferson, James Madison, and James Monroe. However, when the congressional caucus attempted in 1824 to nominate Secretary of the Treasury William

Crawford (even though he was from Georgia, he was Virginian by birth), three-fourths of the Republican congressmen boycotted the meeting. Eventually, five candidates were nominated for president that year, including Andrew Jackson, who was proposed by the Tennessee legislature. In the election that followed, no candidate received a majority of the electoral votes and, as a result, the election was thrown into the House of Representatives. To make matters worse, the House did not choose Jackson—the candidate with the most electoral votes—but John Quincy Adams (still another former secretary of state). Adams benefited from a political deal with Henry Clay, one of the five nominees, who threw his support in the House to Adams in return for being named secretary of state. This unfortunate combination of circumstances discredited the congressional caucus (known as "King Caucus") as a means of nominating presidential candidates.

In 1828 presidential nominations swung completely to the state level as legislatures and conventions chose "favorite sons" such as Jackson and Adams as candidates. However, if the congressional caucus was too centralized to represent the state and local units of the party, selection by individual states was too decentralized to select a national official. Some device was needed that would represent party elements in various parts of the country and, at the same time, facilitate the nomination of a common candidate.

The National Convention

The nomination method that emerged to meet these needs was a genuine national party convention composed of delegates chosen from all the states. A minor party, the anti-Masons, pioneered the way in 1830 by convening a similar assembly. The National Republicans* (who, like the anti-Masons, had no appreciable representation in Congress and thus could not have used the congressional caucus even if they had wanted to) called a similar convention the following year. So did the Democratic Republicans under President Andrew Jackson, who viewed such a convention as an ideal way of getting Jackson's handpicked candidate, Martin Van Buren, chosen by the delegates as vice president.

Since the early 1840s, both major political parties have nominated their presidential and vice-presidential candidates by holding national conventions. Within ten years they began the practice of having their national committees call the presidential nominating conventions into session and of having the convention adopt a platform (David, Goldman, and Bain, 1964: 61). Moreover, as discussed later, the parties retained two of the basic features of these early conventions in modified form: the allocation of delegates to states on the basis of their representation in

---

*This party was soon to give way to the "Whigs," with many Whig supporters joining the Republican party when it was formed in the 1850s.

Congress (senators plus congressmen); and the selection of delegates by each state, using any appropriate means.*

The evolution of the process for nominating the president reflects broader trends and features of American political life. It is closely linked with the development of our two-party system. As the power base of the parties spread from Congress into state and local constituencies, it was necessary to abandon the centralized congressional caucus and to develop some method that would represent persons who were active in party affairs at the grass-roots level. At the same time, the nomination method had to be flexible in order to unite the diverse elements of each party behind a single presidential candidate. The current procedure of calling a national convention for presidential nominations serves both these functions of representation and unification.

The national convention also adapted itself to the American constitutional framework. The congressional caucus, which was more suitable for a parliamentary system than for a presidential system, was discarded in favor of a convention that reflected the separation-of-powers principle. This frees the chief executive from depending on his constitutional rival, the Congress, to nominate him. Moreover, both the allocation of convention votes to states and the practice of permitting each state to choose its delegates by any method it chooses are consistent with the basic features of American federalism.

Finally, the evolution of the presidential nomination process reflects the increasing democratization of American politics. Over the years the trend has been to have more and more people participate in the nomination of the nation's chief executive. As the next section shows, the search for broader popular participation continues to characterize the recent nomination method.

THE DEVELOPMENT OF CURRENT NOMINATION RULES

The rules that govern any political contest are important. On one hand, they shape the process, determining the strategies and tactics that participants follow in order to maximize their chances of winning. On the other hand, rules become the focus of struggles for change as persons seek to write them to favor their particular interests. The prevailing rules are seldom neutral: they inevitably give an advantage to certain individuals and interests over others, even though it is sometimes difficult to predict specific consequences that will occur if existing rules are changed. Thus, rules both prescribe behavior in political contests and help determine their outcomes.

In recent years the rules of the presidential nomination contest have become especially important. They are highly complicated, since they come from a variety

*As indicated later in this chapter, recently the national parties (particularly the Democrats) have begun to regulate the methods by which states choose their delegates to the National Convention.

of sources, including actions of 100 separate state political parties and fifty legislatures, the national political parties, and the Congress. (Sometimes individuals turn
to the courts to interpret provisions of these regulations and to reconcile conflicts
among them.) In addition, the rules have been changed so drastically and so often,
particularly in the Democratic party, that it is difficult for candidates and their
supporters to keep up with the changes. The results have created confusion and
uncertainty for many participants in the nomination process and favored persons
who somehow manage to puzzle their way through the welter of rules that govern
the selection of presidential nominees. Indeed, some persons attribute part of
George McGovern's success in winning the Democratic nomination in 1972 to his
close association with and appreciation of the changes made in the nomination rules
that year.*

A variety of rules governs various stages of the nomination process. Immediately following we will examine two important aspects of such rules: the
apportionment of convention votes among the various states; and the methods states
use in selecting the delegates allocated to them. Later we will look at two other
kinds of rules: provisions that apply to the financing of candidates' campaigns; and
regulations that govern the proceedings of the national convention.

The Apportionment of Convention Delegates

As indicated earlier in this chapter, both political parties initially adopted the practice of allotting convention votes to states on the basis of the size of their congressional delegation (multiplying that number by some constant figure to allow for a
larger number of delegates). They thus incorporated the "Connecticut Compromise" solution that the Founders had used to settle the small-state, large-state
controversy over legislative representation (each state had two senators, but the size
of its House delegation depended on its population) into the presidential nomination
process. This principle also directly tied the nomination procedure to the general
election, since the size of state congressional delegations also determined the
number of votes they cast in the electoral college.

However, the apportionment method failed to reflect whether a state made a
contribution to a party's victory in the general election. The unfairness of the system
was graphically demonstrated in the Republican contest of 1912. The incumbent
president, William Howard Taft, defeated a former GOP chief executive (and his
onetime political mentor), Teddy Roosevelt, at the convention where the delegations of the Southern states (none of which voted Republican in the general
election) delivered their votes to Taft. Subsequently, Roosevelt entered the race as
the candidate of the Progressive party. In the general election that followed, he

---

*As explained later in this chapter, Senator McGovern originally chaired a commission that helped
bring about major changes in the rules for the 1972 Democratic contest.

received more popular and electoral votes than Taft; the Democratic nominee, Woodrow Wilson, won the election with the help of Southern states that voted for their traditional party candidate.

The Republicans reacted to this situation in 1916 and again in 1920, by reducing the number of Southern delegates at their convention. In 1924 they adopted a new system of rewarding additional ''bonus'' votes to states supporting the party's presidential nominee. In 1944 the Democrats began using a similar system of adding extra delegate votes for states voting for their presidential candidates.

Recently, the two parties have developed different criteria for apportioning convention delegates. Republicans continue to use the size of a state's congressional delegation (or electoral college vote) as a major component of their allocation of delegates; the Democrats have used that same measure as well as state populations alone. The Republicans now take into account states voting not only for their presidential nominees, but also for candidates for the Senate, House of Representatives, and the governorship. In contrast, the Democrats are still concerned with state voting for recent presidential candidates alone, but they take into account the total number of popular votes cast in such elections, a consideration ignored by Republicans.

The different apportionment criteria used by the two parties result in their favoring some states over others in their national conventions. The Republican party's allocation of delegates to states based on their two senators, and emphasis on mere electoral victory and not on the number of votes cast for party candidates, means that small states are advantaged by the GOP, particularly one-party states in which that party dominates other elections besides presidential ones. In contrast, the Democrats' stress on the total number of votes cast in presidential elections alone benefits the populous states, most of which tend to be politically competitive.

The allocation formulas that the two parties use also result in different-sized national conventions. At the Republican convention in 1976, there were 2259 delegate votes cast; at the Democratic convention, the count was 3008. Since both parties require their presidential nominee to win a majority of the convention votes (in 1936, Democrats abandoned their previous two-thirds requirement), the figure in 1976 was 1130 for Republican presidential aspirants and 1505 for Democratic contenders.

The Selection of State Delegates

There are three ways of choosing state delegates to the national convention. One is *appointment by party leaders,* such as members of the state central committee, the state party chairman, or the governor, if a party controls that office. None of the states chooses all their delegates in this manner, but a number of them follow this practice to choose their delegates ''at-large'', who represent the whole state instead of a subdivision, such as a congressional district.

The second method of choosing state delegates is the *caucus-convention* system. This was the system used by most states to select their delegates until recently. It typically involves holding caucuses at the lowest political level (usually rural townships, city precincts, or wards) to choose delegates to county and congressional district conventions, which next elect delegates to the state convention. That body, in turn, picks the state's delegates to the national convention. Although this method involves broader participation than the appointive system, party leaders traditionally have been able to control the caucuses and conventions in order to get themselves and their loyal supporters chosen. This control has been accomplished through superior knowledge of party rules and has sometimes involved methods such as calling caucus and convention meetings without proper notice to all interested parties; packing such meetings with ineligible participants; and using parliamentary maneuvers to recognize speakers, rule on motions, and take votes.

The third way of choosing state delegates to the national convention is the *presidential primary*, in which the rank and file participate. The 1904 Republican national convention seated a group of Wisconsin party regulars instead of the members of the Progressive wing of the party led by Governor Robert LaFollette. The following year, the governor's supporters in the legislature passed a law providing for the future selection of the state's delegates to the national convention through election by the voters (Davis, 1967: 26). In taking that step affecting presidential nominations, the Wisconsin legislature was following up its 1903 action, which provided for the use of primaries in choosing nominees for other political offices.

Even though the action instituting the presidential primary was thus part of the larger primary movement of the time, the two types of primaries are very different. In regular primaries, the voters themselves directly choose the party's nominees. However, participants in presidential primaries select the state's delegates to the national convention who, together with delegates of other states, ultimately choose the presidential nominee. Moreover, the provisions of presidential primaries are much more complicated and vary much more from state to state than those that control regular primary elections for other national and state offices.

The complications and variations among state presidential primary laws passed over the years have related to basic matters such as:

1. *Relationship of Delegates to Presidential Candidates.* Delegates have run as ''committed,'' ''favorable,'' or ''uncommitted'' to a candidate.
2. *Expression of Voters' Presidential Preferences.* Some states have allowed voters to express their preference for a presidential candidate entirely separately from their selection of delegates. The results of such preference polls have been binding on the delegates in national convention voting in some states and merely advisory to the delegates in others.
3. *Duration of Candidate Commitment.* If a delegate is committed to a particular candidate, that commitment may be effective for one, two, or three roll-call votes at the convention, until the candidate's convention vote falls

below a certain percentage of the total vote, or until the candidate releases the delegate from that commitment.

4. *Division of States' Delegate Votes.* States have provided for all their votes to be given to the candidate winning a plurality ("winner-take-all" system), for dividing the delegate votes in proportion to the popular votes ("proportional representation" system), for dividing the votes by geographical districts ("district" system), or by a combination of these systems.

5. *Candidate Access to the Ballot.* States have provided for presidential candidates to be placed on the primary ballot by petition (containing a required number of voters' signatures), or by action of special party committees, or by a state administrative official (such as the secretary of state), based on the person's candidacy's being generally advocated or recognized by the national news media.

6. *Candidate Removal from Ballot.* States have provided for candidates' names being removed from the ballot at their request, on their signing an affidavit that they are not candidates for president in any state that year, or they have not provided any means for candidates having their names removed from the ballot.

7. *Voters' Eligibility to Participate in Primary.* States have held "open" primaries that allow people to participate regardless of their party affiliation and primaries that are "closed" to people not affiliated with that party.

8. *Write-in Candidates.* States have both allowed and forbade voters to write in the names of presidential candidates who do not appear on the ballot.

Thus, the traditional rules for choosing state delegates to the national conventions are complex and vary greatly from state to state. There were no clear patterns or trends in the delegate selection process for a long time. After an initial surge in the adoption of presidential primaries (twenty-six states had done so by 1916), the movement reversed itself; between 1917 and 1935, eight states abandoned their primaries (Davis, 1967: 28). In the late 1940's there was a revival of state presidential primary laws, but soon some of them were repealed; as recently as 1968, only sixteen states used primaries in choosing their delegates to the national convention. However, as the following section shows, that situation, along with the methods used to choose delegates in nonprimary states, was soon to change radically in what Austin Ranney (1975: 1) calls "one of the greatest waves of party reform in the nation's history."

Recent Changes in Delegate Selection Rules

Both parties began to change some of the rules of the nomination contest in the mid-1960s (Crotty, 1977: Chap. 8), but the major reforms came after 1968. The reform movement affected several groups as it began to develop. One was the national Democratic party, which radically changed its delegate selection rules and then worked to get each of the fifty state parties to adopt these changes. Although its actions were less drastic, the national Republican party also altered its selection methods and encouraged state parties to follow its lead. Finally, many state legislatures passed new presidential primary laws or made changes in existing ones.

The Democrats. The vast changes the Democratic party made in its procedures after 1968 can be traced to that year's national convention in Chicago. It was an assembly marked by acrimonious debates within the convention hall over the Vietnam war and bloody battles outside the convention arena between war protestors and the police. The 1968 delegates were concerned that much of the chaos of that convention occurred because the regular party organization was impervious to the will of rank-and-file Democrats (Senator Hubert Humphrey won the nomination without entering a single presidential primary, because party leaders favoring him dominated the delegations of the caucus-convention states), so they adopted a resolution requiring state parties to give "all Democrats a full, meaningful, and timely opportunity to participate" in the selection of delegates. Not long after, the Democratic National Committee established a Commission on Party Structure and Delegate Selection under the chairmanship of Senator George McGovern of South Dakota (later replaced by Congressman Donald Fraser of Minnesota after McGovern became a presidential candidate) to assist state parties in meeting that requirement. The commission developed a list of guidelines designed to accomplish that purpose, and it subsequently worked with state parties to see that the guidelines were implemented in time to affect the selection of delegates to the 1972 Democratic convention.

The McGovern-Fraser commission's guidelines brought about major changes in delegate selection in 1972. The traditional influence of party leaders (known as "professionals") was reduced by regulations that forbade them to serve automatically as *ex officio* delegates to the national convention. Their control over caucuses and conventions was also decreased by requirements of written party rules, adequate public notice of all party meetings, and the elimination of proxy voting. At the same time, wider participation of political "amateurs" (persons interested in the presidential contest because of a concern with issues or particular candidates rather than out of loyalty to the Democratic party) was stimulated by guidelines urging states to remove restrictive voter-registration laws so that non-Democrats and unaffiliated voters could become party members; this change assured the latter's involvement in making up candidate slates.

There were two McGovern-Fraser commission guidelines that had an important effect on the 1972 convention and also stirred up antagonism within the Democratic party. The first required that minority groups, women, and young people (those between eighteen and thirty) be represented in state delegations "in reasonable relationship to the groups' presence in the population of the state.'' Although the commission itself noted that this goal was "not to be accomplished by the mandatory imposition of quotas,'' many state parties did adopt a *quota system*. There was a major convention fight over this issue that resulted in a decision not to seat the Illinois delegation, headed by Mayor Daley, because it did not contain an adequate representation of young people, women, and minorities.

The other recommendation of the commission that became a bone of contention at the 1972 convention related to "the fair representation of minority views on presidential candidates.'' This was aimed at the injustices of the California type of winner-take-all primary that awarded all delegates to the candidate who received simply a plurality of the popular vote. However, this guideline was merely "urged" on state parties by the commission instead of being "required" of them (as were some of the others). Since Californians refused to repeal their primary law, the winner-take-all provision was still in effect in June 1972, when Senator McGovern edged out Senator Humphrey by a 45 to 39 percent popular-vote margin. The convention's Credentials Committee evoked the "spirit" of the guidelines by voting to divide the California delegation vote proportionately to the percentage of the primary vote received by each candidate. However, the entire convention decided to follow the "letter of the law" (the actual provisions of the California statute at the time of the primary) and awarded all 271 delegates to Senator McGovern. The votes of these delegates ultimately proved to be decisive in his first-ballot victory at the convention.

The McGovern forces thus prevailed in the presidential nomination contest, but the battle over the commission guidelines led to deep resentment among many groups within the Democratic party. Minority groups such as Italian- and Polish-Americans, who had traditionally supported the party, questioned why *they* were not included in the newly established quotas. Experienced national officeholders (senators and congressmen) and professional party leaders such as Mayors Daley of Chicago and Yorty of Los Angeles were deeply disturbed when they found their places at the convention taken by women, blacks, young people, and other political amateurs who rallied to the McGovern cause. (About 80 to 90 percent of the 1972 delegates were attending their first national convention.) The disaffection of the professionals in the 1972 general election contributed to Senator McGovern's overwhelming defeat by Richard Nixon.

Determined to reunite the party, the Democratic National Committee appointed a new Delegate Selection Commission in 1973 to work out more satisfactory rules for the 1976 presidential contest. Its members worked under the leadership of Baltimore Councilwoman Barbara Mikulski and were assisted greatly by the national chairman, Robert Strauss. The commission managed to devise a set of rules that were acceptable to both the amateurs and the professionals among the party's activists.

The rules developed by the Mikulski commission changed many of the objectionable features of the McGovern-Fraser commission guidelines. The previously mentioned quotas were specifically eliminated in favor of more inclusive "affirmative action plans" whereby each state party undertook to encourage "minorities, Native-Americans, women, and other traditionally under-represented groups to participate and be represented in the delegate selection process and all party affairs." The new regulations were also more favorable to party professionals, since they encouraged the selection of "public officials, party officials, and members of traditionally under-represented Democratic constituencies" as "at-large" delegates. The Democratic National Committee was asked to extend the privilege of attending the national convention (but not voting) to Democratic governors, senators and representatives as well as to its own members. The commission forbade statewide winner-take-all primaries* and required states to use proportional representation in allocating state delegates, establishing a minimum cutoff of 15 percent for candidates receiving votes in both presidential primaries and caucus-convention meetings in order to qualify for delegates.

The Mikulski commission established a Compliance Review Commission to review state delegation and affirmative action plans to ensure that they met the commission requirements. Although the commission experienced some difficulties in getting states to go along with its recommendations—Wisconsin, for example, failed to repeal its "open" primary law and was eventually given a specific exemption from the "closed" primary regulation—the relationship between the commission and the fifty state parties was much better than the one that its McGovern counterpart had experienced four years previously. The new rules also accomplished their desired purpose: unlike the situation during the 1972 convention (described in Chapter 2), there were no significant arguments over the credentials of state delegations, and party unity prevailed at the 1976 Democratic National Convention.

The concern of the Democratic party with delegate selection rules did not end with the activities of the Mikulski commission. Although some of the newer requirements gained a degree of permanence through incorporation in the charter (a form of party constitution) adopted by the Democrats at their midterm conference in 1974, the National Committee also appointed a Commission on Presidential Nomination and Party Structure to review the rules for selecting delegates to the 1980 national convention. The commission, under the leadership of Morley Winograd, the chairman of the Michigan Democratic party, sought to settle differences between party professionals and amateurs similar to those that had plagued the McGovern and Mikulski commissions. However, a new factor became evident: President Carter's supporters on the commission also worked to ensure that the new

---

*The winner-take-all principle, however, was permitted in contests in units no larger than congressional districts. Such "loophole" primaries, utilized by most of the large states in 1976, were banned from occurring in the future by the national convention that year.

rules developed for the 1980 contest would facilitate the renomination of the incumbent president.

The major problem the Winograd commission faced was the implementation of the concept of proportional representation in allocating a state delegation's votes among candidates. The amateurs fought to retain the 1976 minimum cutoff rule, which allowed candidates receiving 15 percent of the votes in presidential primaries and caucus-convention meetings to receive their proportional share of the delegate votes of the state. The president's supporters and most party professionals, who were concerned with dividing delegate votes among too many candidates and hindering consensus on the party's nominee in 1980, favored a rule that would raise the minimum cutoff figure as the campaign progressed so that minor contenders would be eliminated. The matter was compromised by a plan proposed by the commission stating that in caucus-convention states and for the election of at-large delegates in primary states, a minimum cutoff could be set by a state party at no lower than 15 percent and no higher than 20 percent. For the election of delegates at the district level, the cutoff figure would be determined by dividing the number of district delegates by 100 (in a district with five delegates the cutoff would thus be 20 percent).

In June 1978, the Democratic National Committee adopted the commission's plan on proportional representation* intended for the 1980 convention. It also adopted new rules calling for the shortening of the delegate-selection season from six to three months (from the second Tuesday in March to the second Tuesday in June); requiring states to establish candidate-filing deadlines thirty to ninety days before the election; increasing the size of state delegations by 10 percent to permit the selection of state party and elected officials; and limiting participation in the selection process to Democrats, and allowing no exemptions to states such as Wisconsin, which has open primary laws. These provisions represented a victory for party professionals and White House supporters over amateurs who charged that such rules favored the professionals and were also designed to make more difficult challenges to Carter's renomination from potential candidates such as Governor Edmund Brown and Senator Edward Kennedy.

However, the amateurs won out on two other rules adopted by the Democratic National Committee in December 1978. The first requires that state delegations to the 1980 national convention be equally divided between men and women. The second rule bans winner-take-all contests in single-member districts, which was originally favored by professionals and White House supporters; this latter decision means that all districts will have to select several delegates in 1980 and divide them proportioinately among candidates whose support exceeds the minimum cutoff figure.

---

*The committee amended the rule of the minimum cutoff for district delegates to provide that no primary state could establish a figure higher than 25 percent, regardless of the number of delegates elected in a district.

The Republicans. The Republican party has also made some changes in delegate selection, even though its leaders did not face the pressure for reform that the Democratic leaders faced. A Delegate and Organization Committee (known as the DO Committee) chaired by Missouri National Committeeperson Rosemary Ginn recommended some proposals that were carried out when delegates were chosen for the 1976 convention. Some of the provisions were similar to those of the McGovern commission: reducing the traditional influence of party leaders by eliminating them as *ex officio* delegates; regularizing the nomination process by informing citizens how to participate; and maximizing participation by opening primary and convention systems to all qualified citizens.

At the same time, the Republican party has not attempted to regulate the selection of national convention delegates nearly as extensively as the Democrats have. The 1972 Republican National Convention turned down recommendations of the DO Committee to include in future conventions people under twenty-five years old in "numerical equity to their voting strength in a state" and to have one man, one woman, one person under twenty-five, and one member of a minority group on each of the convention's major committees. Subsequently, the party appointed a new committee under the leadership of the late Congressman Steiger of Wisconsin to develop a way of increasing minority participation in the nomination process, but refused to adopt his recommendation that all states be *required* to have "affirmative action plans" approved by the National Committee. Nor have the Republicans moved to abolish winner-take-all primaries. Thus the Republican party has not been as willing as the Democrats to intervene in state decisions involving the selection of delegates to the national convention.

State Primary Laws. Another aspect of the recent reform movement in the rules of the nomination process has been state legislatures' enactment of many new presidential primary laws. In 1968, sixteen states chose their convention delegates using primaries; four years later that figure rose to twenty-three and, by 1976, it was thirty. Meanwhile, the proportion of total national convention delegates chosen in such primaries climbed from 42 to 63 to 75 percent. In the process, the primary replaced the convention system as the dominant method for choosing delegates to the national convention.

Many of the primary laws passed between 1968 and 1976 contain provisions intended to increase the influence of rank-and-file voters over their party's final presidential choice. States with such laws generally encourage delegates running in primaries to indicate which presidential candidate they personally support, so that voters will know how the delegates may be expected to vote at the national convention. Several states also permit voters to show their preferences for president and legally bind delegates to support the preferred candidates for one or more ballots at the convention. Moreover, under several of the new state laws, names are placed on the ballot if their candidacies are advocated or recognized by the national news media. If they want to remove themselves from the race, they must file an affidavit swearing that they are not candidates in any state that presidential election year. This system prevents candidates from choosing which particular state primaries they personally want to enter, thus allowing voters to pass judgment on a broader range of potential nominees than would otherwise be available.

The sudden burgeoning of presidential primary laws between 1968 and 1976 has been attributed to a variety of causes. Among them was the desire to wrest the nomination process from the control of party professionals and to place it in the hands of rank-and-file voters, and to gain economic benefits stemming from the publicity and visitors attracted to a state by a presidential primary. It is also possible that the new rules developed by the McGovern-Fraser commission for caucus-convention proceedings encouraged states to adopt new primary laws. Austin Ranney, a member of that commission, states (1974: 74) that Democratic governors and legislators preferred to go to a presidential primary instead of radically revising their customary methods of conducting caucuses and conventions for other party matters. Jeane Kirkpatrick, another student of the subject, suggests (1977: 10) that traditional party leaders may have chosen primaries as a way around the complex demands of the new rules, or because the leaders opted to let voters make their decision in primaries instead of competing in caucuses and conventions with political amateurs, such as those who supported Eugene McCarthy and McGovern. Thus, the development of certain rules had an effect on other legal regulations affecting presidential nominations. As the next section indicates, the rules may also have an impact on the outcome of the process.

IMPACT OF THE NOMINATION RULES

The rules of a political contest are seldom neutral; they almost always favor one political candidate over another. As James Lengle and Byron Shafer (1976) suggest, such rules are "the indivisible participant" in the contest. Lengle and Shafer's analysis of the impact of the rules on the 1972 nominations and Pomper's (1977b) calculation of their effect on the struggles in the two parties in 1976 illustrate how various regulations help determine the *results and strategies* of the presidential competition.

As discussed previously, the apportionment formula currently used by the Republicans (electoral college vote plus bonus votes for states supporting the party's presidential, senatorial, congressional, and gubernatorial candidates) benefits the smaller states where the party does well in all these races. Pomper identifies those states as ones of the Sun Belt in the Far West, the Southwest, and the South, which tended to support Ronald Reagan over Gerald Ford in the 1976 GOP presidential contest. In contrast, Jimmy Carter was somewhat disadvantaged by the 1976 Democratic apportionment of state delegates, which gave less weight to the southern states, where he was particularly strong, and more to the large, industrial areas of the Northeast and Midwest, which gave comparatively more support to Carter's Democratic opponents.

The method of selection of delegates also affects presidential candidacies. Pomper's 1976 analysis indicates that Ronald Reagan did better in the "new" primary states (those adopting this selection system between 1968 and 1976) and also outscored President Ford in states with the caucus-convention system; Ford's nomination came about because of the convention votes he received from the "old" primary states (those with pre-1968 laws). In New York and Pennsylvania, there were "uncommitted" delegates who eventually followed traditional state leaders and threw their support to the Republican president. On the Democratic side, Carter was especially favored by the "new" primary states; he received about two-thirds of the delegate votes from these states, as compared to one-third of the delegates chosen in the old primary states and in the states using the caucus-convention method of delegate selection.*

The internal division of states' delegate votes also gives an advantage to certain candidates. Lengle and Shafer maintain that George McGovern benefited by the 1972 rules, because most primary states awarded a considerable number of their delegates by legislative districts, a system that favored his candidacy. They contend that reallocating the primary votes under a statewide winner-take-all method would have meant that Senator Hubert Humphrey would have received a plurality of the primary votes,† while a purely proportional representation system would have given an advantage to Governor George Wallace. Pomper's analysis of the 1976 Democratic contest shows that Carter benefited from the system that year and that if a strict system of statewide proportional representation had been used, he would have received less than 40 percent of the delegates of primary states. (This is the approximate figure that students of nomination politics have concluded is necessary to get a candidate's bandwagon rolling to a quick victory at the national convention.) Pomper also concludes that if a winner-take-all principle had been used in all primaries, Ford would have picked up enough votes to have virtually won the nomination on the basis of primary victories alone.

Rules help shape the contest as it unfolds and, eventually, affect the outcome of the nomination. For example, Lengle and Shafer point out that if the 1972 Pennsylvania primary had used the winner-take-all instead of the district system to allocate its votes, the winner, Hubert Humphrey, would have picked up a large bloc of delegates. This would have meant more media attention and financial support, which would have given additional momentum to his campaign. Pomper suggests

---

*These calculations are based on the vote count after the state primaries and caucus-conventions; by the time of the Democratic National Convention, most of Carter's opponents had dropped out of the race, and the uncommitted delegates came over to his side.

†Pomper points out, however, that Lengle and Shafer's analysis is based solely on pre-California primaries and that if the results of that state's primary are taken into account, McGovern would have benefited the most of all the candidates from a winner-take-all approach in the primaries.

that in 1976, if the Massachusetts and New York primaries had been winner take all, the victor, Senator Henry Jackson, might have been the front-runner in the early phase of the nomination contest instead of Jimmy Carter. Moreover, Ford might have quickly defeated Reagan if his early primary wins, especially in New York and Pennsylvania, had brought him all the delegates from these states.

Of course, it is impossible to determine that the developments just mentioned about have actually occurred, because such analyses fail to consider that if the rules had been different in 1972 and 1976, the various candidates might have changed their campaign strategies. The rules of the contest, along with the other factors, shape the nature of the presidential nomination campaign, a subject to which we now turn.

CHAPTER 2

The Nomination Campaign

The selection of a president is a long and complicated process. It is best thought of as a winnowing one in which the nation ultimately chooses from a huge pool of potential occupants of the office (in 1974 Austin Ranney estimated that 80 million Americans met its constitutional requirements),* the person who will serve as president for the next four years. As Ranney emphasizes, the nomination phase is more important than the election stage, because "the parties' nominating processes eliminate far more presidential possibilities than do the voters' electing processes" (71).

EARLY MANEUVERING FOR POSITION

One of the remarkable features of presidential politics is that maneuvering for the nomination begins so early. In fact, it starts nearly as soon as the previous presidential election is over. John Kennedy decided almost immediately after he lost his chance at the vice-presidential nomination in 1956 to run for the presidency in 1960; George McGovern, an unsuccessful presidential candidate in 1968, made a similar decision for 1972 as soon as the 1968 contest was over. And a few days after the

*These include being a "natural born" citizen, at least thirty-five years old, and a resident of the United States for at least fourteen years.

1972 presidential election, Jimmy Carter's staff provided him with plans he should follow in order to win the 1976 Democratic nomination.

Arthur Hadley (1976) calls this political interval between the election of one president and the start of the first state primary to determine the next presidential candidates "the invisible primary." By this he means that a political contest occurs during this time that has many of the features that characterize the contests that eventually take place in the actual state presidential primaries. The major difference between the two types of primaries is that the "invisible" one takes place behind the scenes as far as the general public is concerned, but that American voters are very conscious of the regular primaries.

The invisible primary is a testing ground for the would-be president to determine whether his candidacy is viable. One factor that Hadley emphasizes is a "psychological" one. Is the candidate willing to undergo the grueling process needed to win, which is characterized by extended absences from home, long hours on the campaign trail, and short, sometimes sleepless, nights? Vice President Walter Mondale, an early casualty of the period preceding the 1976 election, withdrew from the presidential race in November 1974 with the following statement: "I found that I did not have the overwhelming desire to be President which is essential for the kind of campaign that is required. . . . I don't think anyone should be President who is not willing to go through the fire. . . ."

An important task for the presidential candidate at this stage is the assembling of a *staff* to plan the strategy of a campaign and of what Hadley calls a *"constituency,"* a larger group of workers who are willing to do the advance work necessary to organize states for the upcoming primary and caucus-convention contests. The two most recent Democratic party nominees benefited from having dedicated supporters who began their organizational activities very early. A full one and one-half years before the Wisconsin primary in April 1972, a young McGovern staff member, Eugene Pokorny, began to build a base of operation there (White, 1973: 127); in early 1975, a Carter staffer, Tim Kraft, was assigned the task of putting together a Carter organization for the Iowa precinct caucuses to be held in January 1976 (Schram, 1977: 8).

An obvious resource that presidential aspirants need is *money*. Traditionally, it has been collected from a few large donors (often referred to as "fat cats"), simply because it has been much easier to collect a sizable amount that way instead of seeking donations from many people. Candidates who found that they could not raise funds in that fashion—such as Senator Fred Harris in 1972—soon had to abandon the race. However, recent campaign finance legislation* has radically

---

*Because of the relationships and comparisons that exist between the financing of the nomination and election of presidential candidates, it is both confusing and redundant to discuss the two matters separately. The entire subject—including the legal regulation of the financing of both the nomination and election of the president—is treated in Chapter 3, which deals with the general election process.

changed this situation. Presidential candidates in 1976 who could raise a total of $5000 in each of twenty states in amounts of $250 or less were eligible to receive matching federal funds (up to a total of $5.5 million); Harris and twelve other Democratic candidates along with Republicans Ford and Reagan, met that condition in 1976. Thus, although money is still important, it is available to more presidential candidates today than in the past.

Another factor in this early phase—and perhaps the most important—is how would-be candidates fare with the *media*. As columnist Russell Baker says, the members of the media are the "great mentioner," the source of name recognition and favorable publicity. Candidates who are ignored because news writers and commentators do not regard them as serious candidates find it almost impossible to emerge as viable presidential possibilities. The media can also kill a candidacy; the inability of Governor George Romney of Michigan to cope with the incessant pressure by newspaper, radio, and television reporters to state his policies on Vietnam (especially his unfortunate remark that he had been "brainwashed" by the American military leadership) is credited with ending his campaign before the first 1968 presidential primary (White, 1969: Chap. 2).

Candidates who do well in the invisible primary exploit the advantages provided by the media. Early in his campaign Carter's staff recommended that he compile a list of important political columnists and editors (such as *New York Times* columnist Tom Wicker and *Washington Post* editor Katherine Graham) and cultivate them by making favorable comments on their articles and columns and, if possible, by scheduling visits with them. Some candidates may also appear in the print media as writers of magazine articles or books, such as Kennedy's *Profiles in Courage,* Nixon's *Six Crises,* and Carter's *Why Not the Best?* They also use television and radio, appearing regularly on shows such as "Meet the Press," "Face the Nation," and "Issues and Answers." They may even use a syndicated radio program or news column of their own, as Ronald Reagan did to advance his political views and, indirectly, his candidacy.

People with presidential ambitions typically take additional steps to enhance their prospects with leaders of their party as well as with the American public. Edmund Muskie, who was nominated for vice president by the Democrats in 1968, began accepting speaking engagements outside his home state of Maine soon after he and Hubert Humphrey were defeated. Jimmy Carter assumed the position of Coordinator of the 1974 Democratic Congressional Campaign, a job that took him to thirty states, where he had the opportunity to get acquainted with Democratic leaders. A trip abroad may also keep candidates in the news and, if they have not had much experience in foreign affairs, help to counteract the charge that they are not knowledgeable in this vital area that consumes so much of the American president's time.

However, not all candidates face identical problems in cultivating party leaders and the American voter. Prominent senators and incumbent vice presidents, whose duties place them in the public eye, do not have to work at making themselves politically visible in the same way as state governors, who are comparative new-comers to public life, and people not presently holding public office do. Since the defeated presidential candidate (called the *titular leader*) is most likely to be in the latter category, it is especially important that political fences are kept mended by maintaining contact with national and local party leaders. Titular leaders who hope to be renominated also generally speak out on public issues as a means of conveying the impression that they remain the leaders of the party out of power.

This stage of the contest, characterized by Donald Matthews (1974) as one in which presidential possibilities emerge and the competitive situation is defined,

Table 2.1 Continuity and Change in Presidential Nominating Politics, 1936–1976

Year	Leading Candidates at Beginning of Election Year	Nominee
Party in power		
1936 (D)	Roosevelt	Roosevelt
1940 (D)	Roosevelt	Roosevelt
1944 (D)	Roosevelt	Roosevelt
1948 (D)	Truman	Truman
1952 (D)	Truman	Stevenson
1956 (R)	Eisenhower	Eisenhower
1960 (R)	Nixon	Nixon
1964 (D)	Johnson	Johnson
1968 (D)	Johnson	Humphrey
1972 (R)	Nixon	Nixon
1976 (R)	Ford[a]	Ford
Party out of power		
1936 (R)	Landon	Landon
1940 (R)	?	Wilkie
1944 (R)	Dewey	Dewey
1948 (R)	Dewey-Taft	Dewey
1952 (R)	Eisenhower-Taft	Eisenhower
1956 (D)	Stevenson	Stevenson
1960 (D)	Kennedy	Kennedy
1964 (R)	?	Goldwater
1968 (R)	Nixon	Nixon
1972 (D)	Muskie	McGovern
1976 (D)	Humphrey[a]	Carter

Source. James Barber (ed.), *Choosing the President* (Englewood Cliffs, N.J.: Prentice-Hall, 1974)), p. 54. The question marks shows that no single candidate led in the polls.
[a]The 1976 information is taken from the January Gallup poll.

helps to prepare the way for the formal nomination process that follows. In many instances, the person who emerges as the front-runner in the invisible primary goes on to win the party nomination. As indicated by Table 2.1, since 1936, the person leading in the Gallup poll at the beginning of the presidential year has almost always been chosen as the nominee in both the party in and out of power (that is, the one holding and the one not holding the presidency).

Table 2.1 also shows, however, that the leading candidates in the party out of power in the 1972 and 1976 elections, Muskie and Humphrey, were replaced by McGovern and Carter, respectively. The fact that the latter two candidates were genuine dark horses (McGovern was favored by 3 percent of the Democrats in January 1972, Carter by 2 percent in 1976) indicates that the nature of the invisible primary may be changing. Although it still serves to eliminate candidates (such as Harris in 1972 and Mondale in 1976), it no longer necessarily determines the eventual nominee. As the next section indicates, the actual state primaries have become more and more important in the nomination process.

CAMPAIGNING IN PRESIDENTIAL PRIMARIES

Aspiring presidential candidates must enter primaries. Not only do three-quarters of the delegates to national conventions come from primary states, but the post-World War II records of both political parties indicate that candidates are expected to test their popularity in presidential primaries. Of the sixteen people chosen in the eight presidential elections that took place from 1948 through 1976, fourteen of them had entered the primaries. And the two exceptions—Adlai Stevenson in 1952 and Hubert Humphrey in 1968—were chosen under unusual circumstances. Stevenson had not really wanted to run against the extremely popular Republican candidate, Dwight Eisenhower, who most political observers considered unbeatable; Humphrey was prevented from entering many state primaries, because President Johnson did not withdraw from the race until March 31, 1968, the same day Humphrey found out about the decision (Chester, Hodgson, and Page, 1969: 7).

The competitive situation for the nomination differs in the parties in and out of power. Incumbent presidents are expected to enter the primaries. Normally there is little difficulty in soundly defeating challengers; however, in 1976 Gerald Ford experienced a genuine challenge from Governor Ronald Reagan, who won in seven of the seventeen primaries in which voters expressed their preferences for a Republican; Reagan actually outscored Ford 51 to 49 percent in the total popular vote cast in those states.* Moreover, in the party out of power, the battle for the nomination is typically spirited, with the party's candidate victorious in the primaries; presidential

---

*Most analysts attribute Ford's difficulties that year to the unusual circumstances under which he took office (he was the first vice president to become president without having been elected to the vice presidency) and to his lackluster performance on the campaign trail as compared to that of Reagan, a former movie star and television personality.

hopefuls who choose to stay out of these contests—such as Democrats Lyndon Johnson (1960) and Hubert Humphrey (1976), and Republicans William Scranton (1964) and Nelson Rockefeller (1968)—watch others walk off with the nomination.

The crucial question for serious presidential contenders is not *whether* they should go into the primaries; instead, it is *which particular ones* they should enter. However, even those options are not as numerous as they once were. The trend in recent state primary laws—automatically entering people in the race if candidacies are generally advocated or recognized by the national media and making it difficult or impossible for them to withdraw—forces candidates into contest in such states. Moreover, candidates are expected to demonstrate their strength in various parts of the country. As a result, in 1976 Jimmy Carter's name appeared on the ballot of twenty-six of the twenty-seven states with presidential preference primaries (the exception was West Virginia, whose favorite son, Senator Robert Byrd, won); following close behind were Wallace in twenty-four states and Udall and Jackson in twenty-two states each.

Of course, having candidates' names appear on a particular state's ballot does not mean that they will wage all-out campaigns there. Limitations of time, energy, and money force presidential aspirants to establish priorities among the many primaries. On one hand, candidates must avoid actively campaigning in so many states simultaneously that their efforts are dissipated and ineffective, as Edmund Muskie's were in the early stages of the 1972 campaign (White, 1973: Chap. 4). Furthermore, candidates must not concentrate on too few states—which is what Nelson Rockefeller did in 1964 when he contested seriously with other major candidates in only three states and lost two of them (White, 1965: Chap. 4).

Candidates take a number of factors into account when deciding which primaries they should emphasize in their nomination campaigns. One is the *time* the primary is held. The earliest contest, traditionally New Hampshire, usually attracts most of the major contenders because it is the first test of popular sentiment. Although its number of delegates is small (17 of the 3008 delegate votes at the 1976 Democratic national convention, 21 of the 2259 at the Republican one), it focuses immediate attention on the winner, as it did for Kennedy in 1960 and Carter in 1976. Moreover, even if a candidate loses in New Hampshire, but draws a greater percentage of the vote than expected, the media may interpret the results as a "moral" victory, a judgment that benefited Eugene McCarthy in 1968 and George McGovern in 1972.

New Hampshire appeals to presidential candidates for another reason: its small area and population make campaigning there a manageable operation. Only about 20,000 Democrats were registered in 1976, and the Carter organization claimed to have contacted about 95 percent of them (Schram, 1977: 20). Thus, the state was ideal for the former governor in the early stages of the nomination contest before he acquired substantial financial resources for media expenditures and when his contingent of Georgia volunteers could conduct an effective door-to-door campaign.

Other primaries provide a late indication of voter preference. The California primary is one example, since it traditionally occurs near the end of the primary season. If the earlier primaries have not produced a clear favorite, the Golden State can determine who the party's nominee will be. Both Goldwater in 1964 and McGovern in 1972 owed their ultimate selection to their primary victories in California, which projected them as "winners," as delegates throughout the country looked toward the upcoming national convention. Moreover, the rules of the nomination contest also make California an attractive target for presidential candidates. California has the largest number of state delegates at each of the party conventions and, for Republicans, a winner-take-all provision that delivers those delegates in a solid bloc to the winner of the primary.

Other factors besides timing and delegate strength affect candidates' decisions about where to concentrate campaign efforts. Naturally, they try to choose states where they think they have the best chance of winning. In 1976, Jimmy Carter campaigned heavily in Florida, not only because its primary was held early in the year, but also because it is next to his home base of Georgia, which was a convenient source for campaign workers. Also in 1976, Henry Jackson chose Massachusetts and New York as special targets because both states contained many Catholics, Jews, and labor-union members with whom the Washington senator felt he had close political ties. Morris Udall zeroed in on Massachusetts and Wisconsin, because he expected to do well in the liberal academic communities concentrated in those states. The two Republican contenders in 1976, Gerald Ford and Ronald Reagan, worked hard in their home states of Michigan and California to advance their candidacies.

The success of a presidential candidate depends on the choices made in the primary campaign. It is much easier to assess the soundness of a "game plan" in retrospect than it is to predict how a given strategy will work out. Nonetheless, there is little doubt that in 1976 Jimmy Carter profited from the following plan (reprinted in Witcover, 1977: 114), laid out for him in a memorandum written by Hamilton Jordan in November 1972, three and one-half years before the primary season began.

1. Demonstrate in the first primaries your strength as a candidate. This means a strong surprise showing in New Hampshire and a victory in Florida.
2. Establish that you are not a regional candidate by winning early primaries in medium-size states outside the South, such as Rhode Island and Wisconsin.
3. Select one of the large industrial and traditionally Democratic states which has an early primary to confront all major opponents and establish yourself as a major contender. Pennsylvania and Ohio would be possibilities.
4. Demonstrate consistent strength in all primaries entered.

(As Witcover notes, the results closely followed the script. Carter won all the aforenamed primaries except Rhode Island, where he ran behind an uncommitted slate; moreover, he won eighteen of the twenty-nine primaries he entered and did not experience a primary night—there were fourteen of them—without a victory in some state.)

However, the results of the primary campaign may depend not only on the winning candidate's making the "right" decisions, but also on opponents making the "wrong" ones. Again using the 1976 Democratic contest as an example, Martin Schram (1977: 198–199) lists a series of "ifs" that might have changed the course of that campaign.

If Udall had been willing, right away, to spend $25,000 on television ads— instead of being off the air entirely during the last crucial weekend in Wisconsin, where he had been making such big gains and wound up just short of defeating Carter.

If Jackson had seen Pennsylvania early on as his big confrontation with Carter, and had planned and organized and spent there accordingly.

If Hubert Humphrey had made a real run early, instead of just sitting on Capitol Hill assessing and reassessing and re-reassessing.

If the liberals had gotten behind one man from the start, rather than siphoning votes from each other.

Of course, this list is merely suggestive and does not exhaust the circumstances that could have turned around the 1976 Democratic contest. For example, what would have happened if Governor Edmund Brown of California—who defeated Carter several times in the later part of the campaign in Maryland, Nevada, and California—had entered the race sooner? As a candidate preaching an anti-"Big Government" theme similar to the one espoused by Carter, might he not have drained off some "conservative" votes that went to Carter in some of the initial primaries? Or what if liberal candidates such as Birch Bayh, Sargent Shriver, and Fred Harris, once they started to lose primaries decisively, had dropped out of the race sooner and publicly endorsed Udall—would that not have helped him in some of the primaries, especially in Massachusetts and Wisconsin, where he placed second? Schram suggests that although it might have been different in 1976, it was not. Carter won mainly because of his own campaign, not because of opponents' mistakes. The presidential candidate who makes judicious choices and campaigns effectively in primaries so that he wins most of them or who scores significant victories in some key contests, goes a long way toward establishing his claim for the nomination. The wise presidential aspirant, however, does not put all his efforts into the primaries; he works to gather as much support as he can from as many sources as possible.

GATHERING DELEGATE SUPPORT IN STATES WITHOUT PRIMARIES

As we have seen, party professionals traditionally dominated the selection of delegates in nonprimary states. Few ordinary citizens took the time and effort to attend the caucuses and conventions at which delegates were selected. Those who did found themselves outnumbered and outmaneuvered by activists in party affairs. As a result, party loyalists were chosen as delegates and took their cues on how to vote at the national convention from the delegation chairman or other influential party leaders in the state who had helped select them. These leaders, in turn, were often willing to bargain their delegation's votes at the national convention for benefits for themselves (a federal appointment) or their state (a public works project); they were also willing to support a compromise candidate who had the best chance of winning in November.

Recently, however, large numbers of political amateurs have been appearing at caucuses and conventions. They have sought to choose delegates committed to candidates on the basis of candidates' stands on issues instead of on the criteria favored by party professionals: acceptability to all elements of the party and ultimate electability. Although the professionals have sometimes prevailed in such contests—as they did on behalf of Hubert Humphrey in 1968—the amateurs have also scored some notable victories. Supporters of George McGovern in 1972 bene-fited from the 1972 Democratic guidelines, which opened up the selection process to broader participation by people who had never been active Democrats. In 1976 conservative enthusiasts for Ronald Reagan won many contests in party caucuses and conventions, as did liberal supporters of Jimmy Carter.

Even though fewer delegates are chosen today from nonprimary states than in the past, contests in those states can still be important in presidential nominations. If no clear-cut verdict on the preferred candidate emerges from the primaries (as in the 1976 Republican contest), the delegates chosen in party caucuses and conventions are in a position to help determine who the nominee will be. Moreover, contenders' performances in such contests may also affect their candidacies in primary states. Many observers considered Carter's initial victory in the Iowa precinct caucuses to have given him a psychological edge in the New Hampshire primary, which took place shortly thereafter.

RECENT TRENDS IN PRECONVENTION POLITICS

There have been significant changes in the presidential nomination contest in recent years. New groups have arisen to supplement and, in some cases, replace, the influence that state party professionals once exercised over the choice of the party nominee. One such group is the *amateurs,* who encourage issue-oriented candidates to become presidential candidates and work very hard for those candidates in primary and nonprimary states. The Goldwater "movement" in 1964, Eugene McCar-thy's college student supporters in 1968, and what Theodore White (1973: 125) terms George McGovern's "guerrilla army" in 1972—groups that spanned the political spectrum from ideological conservatives, to war protesters, to "cultural" liberals—brought a new type of political activist into presidential politics. Jeane

Kirkpatrick (1976) refers to such activists as a "new presidential elite." They are usually part of the upper middle class and have neither the experience in nor the loyalty to traditional party organizations that those groups generally require. The new presidential elite often takes a keen interest in the intellectual and moral aspects of politics and use verbal skills to great advantage in presidential politics.

Another major change in nomination politics is the growth of the importance of the *media*. These include the political reporters and columnists for newspapers such as the *New York Times* and the *Washington Post,* news magazines such as *Time* and *Newsweek,* the wire services, United Press International and the Associated Press and, finally, network television commentators for ABC, CBS, and NBC, all of whom can greatly influence the fate of presidential hopefuls. These people determine who will be taken seriously as candidates, predict who will win the various primaries and caucuses, and interpret, according to the results of these contests, who the "real" winners and losers are compared to how much support media-masters think the candidates will get.* These individuals also decide how much publicity is given to individuals and assess the image, presidential qualifications, and stands on issues of would-be candidates.

Timothy Crouse (1972: Chap. 1), a press participant in the 1972 campaign, calls one of the major features of campaign coverage, "pack journalism." He means that the many reporters who cover the candidates eventually "begin to believe the same rumors, subscribe to the same theories, and write the same stories" (p. 8), and that the representatives of the smaller newspapers (as well as their employers) take their cues mostly from experienced national reporters such as David Broder of the *Washington Post* and R.W. Apple, Jr. of the *New York Times.* Crouse also suggests that a reporter tends to be uncritical of a candidate to whom he is assigned because, if he is writing about a front-runner, he is "guaranteed front-page play for his stories," and if he stays with a winner through the primaries, "he will probably be assigned to follow him through the fall election—perhaps all the way to the White House" (p. 59).

Thomas Patterson (1977), a close student of the 1976 Democratic campaign, points to another basic aspect of media coverage of the nomination campaign: the winner-take-all principle that gives virtually all the publicity, regardless of how narrow the victory or the number of popular votes, to the winning candidate of a state contest. Carter's winning of about 14,000 votes, 28 percent of the 50,000 votes cast in the Iowa precinct caucus (he actually trailed the "uncommitted" group), was interpreted by CBS correspondent Roger Mudd as making Carter a "clear winner" and as opening the "ground between himself and the rest of the pack." (Bayh received 13 percent, Harris 10 percent, Udall 6 percent, Shriver 3

*William Bicker (1978: 93) does report, however, that in 1976 the network executives decided to declare only the candidate who won the most votes as the primary winner instead of announcing "moral" victories.

percent, and Jackson 1 percent). On that basis Carter dominated *Time* and *News-week* coverage of the event and, when he won by a 4000 vote margin in the New Hampshire primary, which involved 77,000 ballots, he made the covers of both magazines. Patterson's analysis of primary election coverage of Democratic candidates by television news, newspapers, and weekly news magazines between the New Hampshire and Pennsylvania primaries showed that Carter received almost half of the publicity; no other candidate received more than 15 percent. Meanwhile, Carter's public recognition by voters grew from 20 percent to 83 percent.

A final development in presidential nomination politics is the increased use of *media consultants, public relations experts,* and *direct mail specialists* who assist candidates by writing speeches, planning campaign strategy, raising money, and getting out the vote. Political pollsters are another important group; they help candidates assess their nomination prospects and provide vital "feedback" on the reactions of voters to their campaigns, the issues that people are thinking about, and attitudes of groups on those issues.

The result of these new developments has been the *popularization* of the presidential nomination contest. Moreover, the various forces affect each other: candidates who receive favorable treatment from the media tend to do well in the primaries which, in turn, raises their standings in the polls. Favorable polls also impress representatives of the media, political activists, and many rank-and-file voters; this results in more victories for the poll leader in nonprimary and primary contests. Presidential contenders who benefit from this reinforcement often gain the necessary support for the nomination before the convention meets. Still, they cannot be sure until then whether promises of votes will be kept. Moreover, as indicated in the following section, the convention serves other purposes for people who have their eyes on the White House.

THE NATIONAL CONVENTION

The national convention is important to presidential candidates for two major reasons. First, whatever may have happened before, the actual nomination occurs at the convention. Second, the convention provides opportunities for candidates to strengthen their chances to win the general election the following November.

A number of decisions that precede the balloting on presidential nominations can have significant effects. Sometimes the location of the convention is important. (This decision is officially made by the National Committee: for the out party, the chairman of the National Committee has the greatest say in the matter; for the in party, the president does.) Illinois governor Adlai Stevenson's welcoming speech to the Democratic delegates assembled in Chicago in 1952 is credited with influencing their decision to nominate him that year. In 1968 the events that grew out of the confrontation between protestors and Mayor Daley's police in that same city contributed to Hubert Humphrey's defeat in the general election.

Contests between rival slates of delegates from states where there have been disputes in the selection process are also important. At the 1952 Republican convention, the Credentials Committee awarded Robert Taft a majority of the delegates in several southern states, but this decision was overturned on the floor of the convention in favor of the ultimate nominee, Dwight Eisenhower (Keech and Matthews, 1976: 183). There were eighty-two separate challenges involving thirty states and over 40 percent of the delegates at the 1972 Democratic convention; most of them stemmed from alleged violations of the McGovern-Fraser guidelines. Eventually, all but two were settled by the Credentials Committee, the fight over the California delegation and another dispute that led to a convention decision not to seat the Illinois delegation, linked with Mayor Daley of Chicago on the grounds that it did not contain an adequate representation of youth, women, and minorities and was chosen through closed, slate-making processes.

Fights over rules of convention proceedings sometimes take on great significance. One of these battles occurred at the 1976 Republican convention when the Reagan forces moved to amend the rules to require candidates to name their vice-presidential choice in advance of the balloting on presidential candidates, hoping thereby to force Ford to name a running mate and thus risk the loss of supporters who would be disappointed with his decision. (Before the convention Reagan had chosen liberal Pennsylvania senator Richard Schweiker as his vice president, a move calculated to bring him needed support from uncommitted delegates in large eastern states such as New York and Pennsylvania.) The defeat of that amendment helped pave the way for President Ford's victory on the first ballot that year.

Writing and adopting the party platform is another major convention decision. Although these documents have traditionally been ridiculed as containing promises the party does not intend to keep or as including vague phrases produced by the necessities of compromise, the fact is that many delegates and party leaders have taken them seriously (Parris, 1972: 110). In 1948 some southern delegations walked out of the Democratic convention because they felt that the platform was too liberal on the issue of civil rights; twenty years later the delegates of the same party debated the Vietnam plank of the platform before a nationwide television audience in an astonishing display of self-criticism by the party in power.

Republicans have also had their share of platform disputes. In 1960 Nelson Rockefeller threatened to lead a floor fight over the platform unless it committed the party to stronger programs for national defense and civil rights. To avoid that fight, Richard Nixon agreed to Rockefeller's demands and used his influence to include the changes in the platform. In 1976 the Ford supporters pursued a similar course of action by not contesting a platform amendment suggested by Reagan supporters criticizing the U.S. policy of détente with the Soviet Union. However, in 1964, the Goldwater forces used the opposite tactic by refusing to make any concessions to party liberals such as Governors Rockefeller of New York and Romney of Michigan on the issues of civil rights and political extremism.

Credentials contests, adoption of rules of procedure, and the party platform are tests of strength for potential presidential candidates and also provide opportunities for forging the kinds of political alliances needed to win the nomination. However, they have other effects. Ronald Reagan lost the Republican nomination in 1976 to President Ford, but he was successful in getting many of his conservative ideas incorporated in the GOP platform.* The statement of party principles may also influence the general election campaign, since party leaders who oppose them may not be inclined to work very hard on the party's behalf. Republican Governors Rockefeller and Romney did little to help Goldwater in 1964, and many Democrats opposed to the proadministration plank on Vietnam in the party's 1968 platform did not rouse themselves in the general election campaign that year. In 1972 many conservatives and centrists in the party who were unhappy with the Democratic platform, which included stands on amnesty for war resisters and school busing that were much more liberal than the sentiments of the average American (Sullivan, Pressman, and Arterton, 1974: 107), refused to work for McGovern in the fall.

Although candidates must be concerned with such matters during the early stages of the convention, they and their supporters must work together toward the crucial decision of the meeting: the balloting that normally occurs on the third or fourth day of the proceedings. In the interim, preparations are made for the roll-call vote. Presidential hopefuls call on caucuses of state delegations and, also, individual delegates to solicit support. Polls are taken of delegates so that candidates know how many votes they can count on and from whom they might pick up additional support. In 1960 Edward Kennedy retained contacts with the Wyoming delegates he had worked with the previous spring and was in their midst when their votes won his brother the nomination on the first ballot (White, 1961: 203). Also in 1960, Richard Nixon arranged to have his picture taken with each delegate at the Republican convention (Polsby and Wildavsky, 1964: 82).

The kind of strategy candidates employ in the balloting for the nomination depends on the amount of delegate support they have. If he is the front-runner, as President Ford claimed he was in 1976, he concentrates on holding the votes he has been promised and on picking up any additional votes needed to win a majority on the initial ballot. The candidates and their workers use the *bandwagon* technique to achieve this goal—that is, they argue that since they are going to win the nomination anyway, delegation chairpersons or individual members who are politically smart will come out now for his candidacy and not wait until the matter has already been settled. The candidate, it is suggested, will remember early support in the future when he is in a position to do political favors. Franklin Roosevelt did so quite

---

*The only platform issue the Ford leaders fought for that year was the Equal Rights Amendment (Weinberg, 1978), which was very strongly supported by the Republican Women's Task Force and the National Federation of Republican Women (Pressman, 1978).

specifically after he was elected in 1932 by determining whether a person seeking a political position backed him "before Chicago," where the convention had been held.

Candidates with weak delegate support attempt to counter the bandwagon technique with their own strategies. Typically, they encourage delegates who do not support them to cast their ballots for favorite sons or other minor candidates. The important thing is to hold down the vote for the front-runner on the first roll call. Candidates also attempt to force alliances to stop the leader. For example, they may agree that at some time during the balloting, those who fall behind in the voting will throw their support to others. The difficulty with making such an arrangement is that minor candidates may frequently have greater differences among themselves than either has with the leader. The only alliance that might conceivably have stopped Richard Nixon at the 1968 Republican convention would have been one between Nelson Rockefeller and Ronald Reagan. However, given their divergent views on vital issues of the day, plus Rockefeller's failure to support Goldwater in 1964 (Reagan had made the best speech of that campaign on Goldwater's behalf), the two governors were hardly a compatible political combination.

The leader, along with minor candidates, offers various enticements in bargaining with possible political supporters. Some people are interested in getting the party to take a particular stand in the platform. Others have more tangible concerns: senators or governors may seek the candidate's support in their own campaigns; other political leaders may be looking toward a cabinet post. Although a presidential candidate himself may refuse to make such commitments so that he can go before his party and the electorate as a "free" man beholden to no one, his supporters do not hesitate to make promises. One delegate to the 1960 convention claimed to be the nineteenth person to whom the Kennedy forces had offered the vice-presidency (Polsby and Wildavsky, 1976: 144).

A definite trend in recent conventions is an early victory for the candidate who arrives at the convention with the greatest number of pledged delegates. In the sixteen conventions that the two major parties have held since World War II, only two nominees—Thomas Dewey in 1948 and Adlai Stevenson in 1952—failed to win a majority of the convention votes on the very first ballot. Thus, the convention has become a body that typically legitimizes the decision on the presidential nominee that has already been made by the time the delegates gather to officially choose a candidate.

The selection of the vice-presidential nominee is the final decision of the convention. Although in theory the delegates make the choice, as a matter of political custom they allow presidential nominees to pick their own running mates. On rare occasions nominees may decide against expressing their own preferences and thus permit the convention to make an open choice, as Adlai Stevenson did in 1956. However, the typical presidential nominee confers with leaders whose judgment he trusts and, when he makes his decision, the word is passed on to the delegates. Even though some delegates may resist a particular vice-presidential candidate, nominees generally get their way. In 1940 Franklin Roosevelt threatened to refuse to accept the presidential nomination unless Henry Wallace was chosen as his vice president. In 1960 John Kennedy insisted on Lyndon Johnson as his running mate over the objections of some liberal elements of the party, including his brother Robert. In effect, the vice president is the winning presidential candidate's first political appointment.

Various considerations underlie the choice of a vice presidential candidate. In the past there has been an attempt to balance the ticket—that is, to select a person who differs in certain ways from the presidential nominee. For example, the two candidates may come from separate parts of the country. The Democratic party often chose Southerners to run with presidential nominees who were typically from other, two-party areas; the Kennedy-Johnson ticket in 1960 was such a combination. In 1976 when a Southerner, Jimmy Carter, won the Democratic presidential contest for the first time since before the Civil War, the process worked in reverse: he chose Senator Walter Mondale from the northern state of Minnesota as his running mate. In 1972 Senator Thomas Eagleton was originally chosen by George McGovern to run with him (as we will see, he was ultimately forced off the ticket), because he possessed certain characteristics the South Dakotan lacked: affiliation with the Roman Catholic church, ties to organized labor, and previous residence in a large city (St. Louis). The ticket is balanced in these ways to broaden its appeal in order to strengthen the party's chances in the general election.*

There are indications, however, that some presidential candidates are at least considering how the vice presidential candidate will perform in office. The trend toward assigning the second in command important responsibilities has led some candidates to choose people with whom they feel they can work effectively as their running mates. This was the main reason why Carter chose Walter Mondale over a number of other northern liberal senators he had personally interviewed for the position, including Edmund Muskie of Maine, Frank Church of Idaho, John Glenn of Ohio, and Adlai Stevenson III of Illinois. The possibility of succession to the highest office has also led presidents to choose running mates who they felt would best be able to step into the presidency if anything should happen to them. There is evidence that John Kennedy regarded Lyndon Johnson as the most capable leader among his rivals for the presidential nomination in 1960.

These factors are not mutually exclusive. It is possible to choose someone for the second place on the ticket because of more than one of these considerations. Thus, Kennedy also chose Lyndon Johnson because he calculated that Johnson's

---

*Carried to the extreme, the balancing principle would lead to the selection of a candidate who differs in many respects from the presidential nominee. One wag suggested in 1960 that what Richard Nixon needed for a running mate was a Negro nun from the South who was president of a labor union!

presence on the ticket and his campaign efforts in the South would help the Democratic party's chances in that region.

Whatever the considerations are that prompt a presidential nominee to choose a running mate, there is no doubt that the decision is often made too quickly and frequently without complete knowledge of the candidate's background. A classic case occurred in 1972, when McGovern and his staff met the morning after his nomination (many of them having had only two or three hours' sleep) and, by five o'clock that afternoon, finally settled on Senator Thomas Eagleton. The Missourian accepted the nomination after several other people had either turned it down, could not be contacted, or were vetoed by key McGovern supporters. During that time, no one turned up the information on Eagleton's past experiences with mental illness that ultimately led McGovern to force him off the ticket.

The choice of the vice-presidential nominee is the last major decision of the national convention. The final night of the proceedings is given over to acceptance speeches. It is a time for attempting to bring back together the various candidates and party elements that have confronted each other during the long preconvention campaign and the hectic days of the convention. Major party figures are usually expected to come to the convention stage to pledge their support for the winner in the upcoming campaign. At times, however, personal feelings run too high and wounds fail to heal sufficiently for a show of party unity. Important members of the liberal wing of the Republican party in 1964 and many McCarthyites among Democrats in 1968 (including the candidate) refused to endorse the chosen nominee, Hubert Humphrey, at least immediately. In 1972 prominent Democratic leaders, including George Meany of the AFL-CIO, did not support McGovern. Thus the convention does not always achieve one of its main objectives: rallying the party faithful for the general election battle, a subject we will examine in Chapter 3. However, we will conclude this discussion of presidential nominations by analyzing how people participate in the process.

PARTICIPATION IN THE NOMINATION PROCESS

As we will discuss in Chapter 4, how people vote in presidential elections has become a major focus of scholarly interest, particularly since the end of World War II. In contrast, relatively little attention has been paid to participation in the nomination of the president. This is somewhat surprising, since more candidates are eliminated in this phase of the selection of the president, and thus voters can have more influence at that time than when they choose between nominees of the two major parties in the general election.

In the last decade, however, some studies have appeared that deal with voter participation in the nomination process. These studies concentrate on the incidence of voting in presidential primaries and the factors that affect voter turnout. There is a limited amount of information available on voter participation in the caucus-convention states* and on the reasons why one candidate is chosen over another in presidential primaries.

Trends in Presidential Primary Turnout

As previously indicated, the number of states holding presidential primaries was stable through the 1968 election. However, beginning in 1972 and continuing in 1976, more and more states adopted such contests to choose their national convention delegates. Table 2.2 contains information on voting in presidential primaries since World War II and shows the general effect that additional primaries had on the total primary turnout. The number of persons participating in the presidential primaries jumped from 12 million to 22 million between 1968 and 1972 and rose again in 1976 to over 26 million, more than twice the primary electorate in 1968.

Table 2.2 also shows that major differences have occurred between the two parties in their primary turnout over the period analyzed. The Republicans held the edge over the Democrats in 1948 and again in 1952, when Senator Taft and General Eisenhower contested in a series of presidential primaries. However, since 1956 the situation is reversed; more Democrats vote in presidential primaries than Republicans. The disparity was especially apparent in the 1972 election, when a number of Democrats fought it out in the primaries but the incumbent president, Richard Nixon, had little difficulty being renominated by the Republicans.

Although Table 2.2 provides general information on participation in presidential primaries, the data do not indicate how much of the increased turnout in recent years is a result of more states conducting primaries in 1972 and 1976 than they did in earlier years. Nor do the data reveal how many interparty differences in turnout can be attributed to the possibility that more people may have identified with the Democrats instead of the Republicans in the primary states, which meant that the Democrats had a larger pool of potential partisans from which to draw than the Republicans.

Figure 2.1, developed by Richard Rubin (forthcoming), takes these problems into account by computing turnout as a percentage of the number of persons who were registered to vote in each party in the states that held closed primaries† from 1948 to 1976. It shows that the increase in primary voting among Republicans and Democrats between 1968 and 1972 did not occur simply because more states held primaries in 1972; instead, a larger percentage of the eligible voters in both parties

---

*On the basis of information gathered from Democratic state organizations, *Congressional Quarterly Weekly Report,* July 10, 1976, p. 1809, states that nearly 760,000 Democrats participated in caucuses held in twenty-two states and four territories in 1976. The best turnout rate was in Connecticut, where 1 percent of the registered Democrats participated.

†Recall that closed primaries are restricted to persons affiliated with a particular party; open ones allow persons to participate, regardless of party affiliation.

Table 2.2 Number of Presidential Primaries and Primary Votes Cast, 1948–1976

Year	Number of Primaries Held		Votes Cast in Primaries		
	Republican	Democratic	Republican	Democratic	Total
1948	12	14	2,653,255	2,151,865	4,805,120
1952	13	15	7,801,423	4,907,225	12,710,638
1956	19	19	5,828,272	5,832,592	11,660,864
1960	15	16	5,537,967	5,686,664	11,224,631
1964	16	16	5,935,339	6,247,435	12,182,774
1968	15	15	4,473,551	7,535,069	12,008,606
1972	20	21	6,188,281	15,993,965	22,182,246
1976	30	30	10,374,125	16,052,652	26,426,777

Source. Congressional Quarterly, Presidential Elections Since 1789, Washington, D.C., 1975, pp. 138–155. The 1976 data are from Congressional Quarterly Weekly Report, September 24, 1977, p. 2042.

cast their ballots in the 1972 contest than in the 1968 primaries. Table 2.2 also indicates that even though the proportion of registered Republicans who participated in presidential primaries continued to rise between 1972 and 1976, the voter turnout rate for Democrats declined.

As far as overall turnout of eligible voters is concerned (that is, accounting for the rate of participation in both parties), there was some falloff in participation in the 1976 presidential primaries. Austin Ranney (1976: 22) considers the decline significant, particularly since there were many closely contested primaries that year. Rubin interprets the situation differently, noting that there was not a close challenge to Carter after the Pennsylvania primary (the ninth out of thirty primaries), and that the large number of new state contests involved voters who had not yet been socialized into participating in presidential primaries. Rubin feels that under these circumstances, participation in the 1976 presidential primaries was relatively high.

Factors Affecting Turnout

Analyses of voting in presidential primaries indicate that the most important factor affecting turnout in such contests is *political competition* (Zeidenstein, 1970; Ranney, 1972; Morris and Davis, 1975; Jewell and Olson, 1978). Turnout is generally greater in primaries with two or more candidates than in those in which only one presidential candidate is entered or where only "write-in" names are added to the ballot. The closeness of the contest also makes a difference, as does the entrance of a national contender into a contest. Finally, the larger the number of candidates on the ballot, the greater the turnout tends to be.

Another political factor that affects participation in presidential primaries is

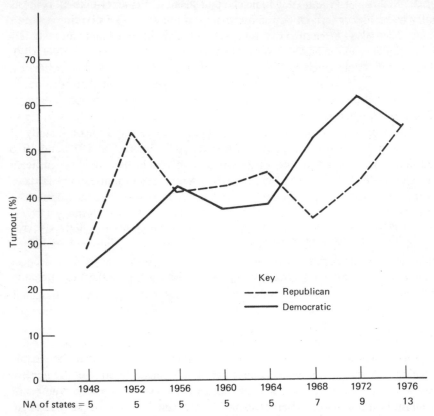

Figure 2.1. Turnout of registered voters by party in closed presidential preference primaries, 1948 to 1976. [Source: Richard Rubin "Presidential Primaries: Continuities, Dimensions of Change, and Political Implications," in William Crotty, ed., *The Party Symbol* (San Francisco: *W. H. Freeman & Company, forthcoming).*

campaign spending. Ranney (1976: 32–33), in his analysis of the 1976 primaries, found that the higher the percentage of the legal spending limits that three leading candidates (Jimmy Carter, Gerald Ford, and Ronald Reagan) spent as a group in a state, the greater the turnout in that state was. A separate test of the effect of the spending by just Ford and Reagan in the Republican primaries alone produced the same general result.

Certain *legal provisions* of presidential primaries also affect voter turnout. For example, both Zeidenstein and Ranney (1976) found that participation tends to be higher in states with presidential preference polls that bind delegates at the national convention. Morris and Davis' analyses of voting in Democratic presidential primaries in 1964, 1968, and 1972 indicated that states with winner-take-all contests generally had a higher turnout than those that used other ways of dividing a state's delegates. They also determined that turnout was higher in states that automatically entered candidates on the ballot (instead of depending on them to enter voluntarily), a finding that was confirmed by Ranney's study of the 1976 presidential primaries. Finally, Ranney's 1976 analysis indicated that more people tended to turn out in states with closed presidential primaries as compared to those with open contests.

The effect of permitting voters to participate in such open contests has also been analyzed by students of presidential primaries. Jewell and Olson's study of participation in Tennessee and Michigan presidential primaries in 1972 and 1976 showed that voters tended to shift to the primary in which there was a significant contest. George Wallace's presence in the 1972 Democratic primaries in both states drew voters but, with Wallace absent in 1976, they tended to shift to the Republican primaries in which Ford and Reagan were contesting. Similarly, Ranney (1972), Adamany (1976), and Hedlund and Watts (1977) reveal a shifting of both partisans and independents in the Wisconsin open presidential primary; voters were attracted to candidates who had special personal or ideological appeal for them instead of being motivated to "raid" the primary to cast a ballot for the weakest candidate in the party for which they did not normally vote.

Representativeness of Presidential Primaries

Some years ago V.O. Key (1956: Chap. 5) expressed concern that the people participating in primaries for state offices might not be representative of the general membership of the party. He raised the possibility that an especially large number of voters might turn out to vote for local officials in particular areas of party strength (such as cities and counties); at that same election they would cast their ballot in nominations for statewide offices, which would mean that they would have a disproportionate effect in such races. He went on to speculate that the primary constituency might consist predominantly of persons of a certain ethnic or religious affiliation or of those especially responsive to a certain style of political leadership or ideology. Key felt that if such possibilities did occur, the unrepresentative nature of the primary constituency might handicap the party in polling its maximum strength in a general election.

We have relatively few studies about the kinds of people who participate in state presidential primaries. Zeidenstein's analysis of nine contests in four states (Illinois, New Hampshire, Oregon, and West Virginia) failed to show that voters in one-party counties participated proportionately more in presidential primaries than they did in presidential general elections. Rubin's study of 1976 voting in three state primaries (Michigan, Ohio, and California) indicated that turnout was lower in urban areas than in suburban and rural ones; however, because of the way convention delegates were apportioned within the state (on the basis of Democratic turnout in the general election), the urban residents were overrepresented (that is, had to cast fewer votes per delegate) as compared to their suburban and rural counterparts.

Austin Ranney's (1972) analysis of the participants in the 1968 New Hampshire and Wisconsin presidential primaries demonstrated that they differed in many ways from partisans who did not vote in those state primaries. The primary voters were older, of higher status in income and occupation, and more active in a variety of civic, religious, and political organizations. Those who voted in the New Hampshire primary also held dissimilar views from nonvoters on several national political issues. For example, the participants tended to be more hawkish on the Vietnam war than nonparticipants. There were also differences in candidate preferences; in New Hampshire and Wisconsin, Democratic primary participants were more pro-President Johnson than nonvoters were.

These limited studies thus indicate that participants in presidential primaries differ in some important respects from partisans who do not vote. Moreover, the primary selectorate is much smaller than the electorate. On the average, about twice as many people vote in the presidential general election as vote in their state's presidential primary (Ranney, 1976: 24–25). For the candidate who wins his party's nomination, this means that he must extend his political appeal to a whole new group of voters. This is the subject we will discuss in Chapter 3.

3

Election Rules and the Presidential Campaign

After the nomination phase of the electoral contest is over, the party designates face a whole new series of political problems associated with winning the general election. Although the rules for the election are not as complicated as those observed during the nomination process, they do favor certain groups of voters over others; thus astute presidential contenders must take this electoral favoritism into account when they plan their fall campaign. That campaign also reflects other new elements such as different provisions for obtaining and spending money to elect candidates and the use of party labels and organizations in the electoral contest. Finally, the audience of the campaign must be broadened to include persons and groups that were not involved in the nomination struggle. Reaching this additional audience is made especially difficult because it must be accomplished in a much shorter time than is available for the nomination process; the general election campaign typically begins around Labor Day and ends two months later on Election Day.

THE RULES OF THE ELECTION CONTEST: THE ELECTORAL COLLEGE

The method of selecting the president was among the most difficult problems faced by the delegates to the Constitutional Convention (Farrand, 1913: 160). A variety of plans were proposed, the two most important being selection by the Congress and direct election by the people. The first, based on the practice in most states of having the governor chosen by the legislature, had the backing of a number of delegates, including Roger Sherman of Connecticut. It was eventually discarded because of the fear of legislative supremacy, and also because the delegates could not choose between state-unit voting, which favored the small states, and joint action of the two chambers, which benefited the large states with their greater voting power in the House of Representatives. Direct popular election was supported by three of the most influential members of the convention—James Madison of Virginia and James Wilson and Gouverneur Morris of Pennsylvania—but it was considered too democratic by most delegates; as George Mason of Virginia put it, "It would be as unnatural to refer the choice of a proper magistrate to the people as it would to refer a trial of colors to a blind man."

Having decided against both popular election and selection by legislative bodies, the delegates proceeded to adopt an entirely new plan put forth by one of their own committees. The proposal, which some historians believe was based on a method used by Maryland to elect its state senators (Peirce, 1968: 43), stated that each state legislature could choose, by whatever means it desired, electors (none of whom could be congressmen or hold other national office) equal to its total number of senators and representatives in Congress. The individual electors would assemble at a fixed time in their respective state capitals and cast two votes each for president. These votes were then to be transmitted to Washington, D.C., where they would be opened and counted during a joint session of Congress. Whoever received the largest number of electoral votes would be declared president, provided a majority (one over half) had been obtained; if no candidate received a majority, the House of Representatives, voting by states (one state delegation, one vote), would choose the president from among the five candidates receiving the highest number of electoral votes. After the president was chosen, the person with the next highest number of electoral votes would be declared vice president. If two or more contenders received an equal number of electoral votes, the Senate would choose the vice president from among them.

This complicated procedure reflected certain values and assumptions about human nature that are enunciated in *The Federalist Papers*.* As previously mentioned, the Founders felt that the average person did not have the ability to make sound judgments about the qualifications of the various presidential candidates; therefore, this crucial decision should be left to a small group of electors—a political elite who would have both the information and the wisdom necessary to choose the best people for the nation's two highest offices. Since the electors could not be national officeholders with connections to the president, they could approach their task without bias; because they assembled separately in their respective state capi-

---

*The particular selection is Number 68, which is generally attributed to Alexander Hamilton. It is difficult to determine whether the views expressed represent the atittudes of a majority of the convention delegates or particularly those of Hamilton, who was more of an elitist than most of the others.

tals rather than as a single body, there would be less chance of their being corrupted or exposed to popular unrest. Moreover, since they were convened for a single purpose and would be dissolved when their task was completed, the possibility of tampering with them in advance or rewarding them with future favors was eliminated.

Philosophy shaped the presidential selection process adopted by the delegates, but so did a recognition of political factors. Lucius Wilmerding (1958: Chap. 8) suggests that some of the delegates did not expect the electors to be entirely insulated from popular preferences on presidential candidates. They rather anticipated that each state's electors would cast one vote for a "native son," a locally popular political figure, and the other for a "continental character," an individual with a national reputation that members of the political elite would be aware of, even though the person might not be well known to the average citizen.* It was also expected that after George Washington's presidency, the electoral votes would be so widely distributed that few candidates would receive a majority and, therefore, most elections (Mason estimated about nineteen out of twenty) would ultimately be decided by the House of Representatives. The electors would thus serve to "screen" (today we would say "nominate") the candidates, and the House would choose (elect) the President from among them. The large-state/small-state conflict that was settled by the Connecticut Compromise on the composition of the Senate and House also arose in the plan the delegates worked out for the selection of the chief executive. In the initial vote by the electors the large states had the advantage, since the number of each state's votes reflected the size of its House delegation. If no candidate got a majority, the small states were favored in the secondary selection, since the contingent vote was by states, not by individuals, in the House of Representatives.

As was true of so many issues decided by the Founders, the method of selecting the president thus represented a compromise. In addition to resolving the large-state/small-state conflict just discussed, the electoral college device took into account the attitudes of states rights' advocates by allowing the state legislatures to decide how the electors should be chosen. It also held open for those who favored letting the people choose the president the possibility of the electors actually reflecting the popular vote for the president in their state. As John Roche (1961: 810) has pointed out, the intermediate elector scheme gave "everybody a piece of the cake"; however, as he also notes, "the future was left to cope with the problem of what to do with this Rube Goldberg mechanism" (p. 811).

As indicated in Chapter 1, events soon nullified both the philosophical and political assumptions underlying the Founders' vision of the electoral college and

---

*Evidence for this assumption is provided by Article II, Section 1 of the Constitution, which states that at least one of the two persons for whom an elector votes must not be an inhabitant of his own state.

forced them to cope with the "Rube Goldberg mechanism." The formation and organization of political parties in the 1790s proceeded so quickly that by the election of 1800, the electors no longer served as independent people exercising their own judgments on candidates' capabilities; instead, they acted as agents of political parties and the general public. In 1800 party discipline was so complete that all Republican electors cast their two votes for Thomas Jefferson and Aaron Burr. Although it was generally understood that Jefferson was the Republican candidate for president and Burr was the candidate for vice president, the Constitution provided no means for the electors to make that distinction on their ballots. The result was a tie in electoral votes between them; neither won a majority (one vote over half of all the votes), and the matter was handed to the House of Representatives for a final decision. Ironically, the Federalists, despite their major defeat in the congressional elections of 1800, still controlled the lame duck Congress (which did not expire until March 1801) and therefore were in a position to help decide which Republicans would serve as president and vice president. At the urging of Alexander Hamilton, who disagreed with Jefferson on policy matters but distrusted Burr personally, some of the Federalist representatives eventually cast blank ballots, which permitted the Republican legislators to choose Jefferson as president on the thirty-sixth ballot.

One result of this bizarre chain of events was the ratification in 1804 of the Twelfth Amendment, stipulating that electors cast separate ballots for president and vice president. The amendment also provides that if no presidential candidate receives a majority of the electoral votes, the House of Representatives, balloting by states, will select the president by majority vote from among the three (instead of the five) candidates who receive the highest number of electoral votes. If no vice-presidential candidate receives a majority of electoral votes, similar procedures are to be used by the Senate in choosing between the two persons with the highest number of electoral ballots.

Other changes in the selection of the president followed; however, they did not come by way of constitutional amendments, but as political developments that fit within the legal framework of the electoral college. Thus state legislators, who were granted the power to determine how electors should be chosen, began giving this right to the general electorate. By 1832 all states except South Carolina had done so.

Another matter left to the discretion of the states—how their electoral votes would be counted—soon underwent change. Initially, states were inclined to divide the vote by congressional districts; the candidate who won the plurality of the popular votes in each district received its electoral vote, and the remaining two electoral votes (representing the two Senate seats) were awarded to the statewide popular winner. However, legislatures soon began to adopt the "unit," or "general ticket," rule whereby all the state's electoral votes went to the candidate who received the plurality of the statewide popular vote. Two political considerations prompted this decision. The state's majority party benefited because it did not have to award any electoral votes to a minority party that might be successful in individual congressional districts. Also, it maximized the influence of the state in the presidential election by permitting it to throw all its electoral votes to one candidate. Once some states adopted this procedure, others, wanting to maintain their political effect on the presidential contest, felt that they had to follow. As a result, by 1836, the district plan had vanished and the unit system taken its place.*

One other major political development of the era changed the nature of the presidential election contest: the elimination on a state-by-state basis of property qualifications for voting. As we will see in Chapter 4, by the early 1840s, *white manhood suffrage* was virtually complete in the United States. Therefore the increasing democratization of American political life is reflected in the procedure for choosing the most important public official. Yet the formal provisions of the electoral college remain the same today as they were in 1804, when the Twelfth Amendment was adopted.

Today these formal provisions provide a strange system for choosing the chief executive. Although most Americans view the system as a popular election, it really is not. When we mark our ballots for a presidential candidate, the vote is actually cast for the electors who are linked with that candidate. In mid-December the state electors associated with the winning candidate (party faithfuls who are chosen in primaries, conventions, or by state committees) meet in their state capitals to vote. (About one-third of the states attempt by law to bind the electors to vote for the winner, but there is some question whether such laws are constitutional.) The results of the electoral balloting are transmitted to Washington, D.C. and, on the following January 6, they are counted and the outcome is announced before a joint session of the Congress by the presiding officer of the Senate—the incumbent vice president. If, as usually happens, one candidate receives a majority of the electoral votes, the vice president officially declares that candidate to be president, a procedure that has occasionally resulted in some ironical moments. In January 1961 Richard Nixon declared his opponent, John Kennedy, to be president; eight years later, another vice president, Hubert Humphrey, declared his political opponent, again Richard Nixon, as the chief executive!

The electoral college system as it operates today is considered not only strange but also grossly unfair and even dangerous by many students of presidential elections. We will assess the various arguments for and against the college in the final chapter but, for the moment, we will restrict our analysis to the interests that are benefited or harmed by the present arrangements, a major consideration for candidates in planning their campaign strategies.

The electoral college today advantages two kinds of states. One is the *small state*, which benefits because all states, regardless of size, receive two electoral

---

*It should be noted that the district plan has been used since that time by a few individual states, most recently by Maine.

votes that represent their two senators. This factor, plus the additional vote they receive for their House member, means that they control three electoral votes, even though their population alone might otherwise entitle them to just one or two votes. However, the very *large states* have even more of an advantage, because they benefit from the unit or general ticket system in which all the electoral votes go to the candidate who wins a simple popular plurality (more votes than anyone else) in the state. Thus, in the 1970s, the popular-vote winner in California received 45 electoral votes, 15 percent of the total of 270 electoral votes required for election.

As far as voters themselves are concerned, the electoral college favors those who reside in states where the competition in presidential elections is close (hence the individual's vote might determine which candidate wins the statewide plurality) and that also have a large number of electoral votes (which may decide which candidate receives the required 270 electoral votes). Calculations by Lawrence Longley (1977), based on the mathematical theory of games and computer simulations of thousands of elections, indicated that in the 1970s a resident of California had more than two and one-half times the voting power of the most disadvantaged citizen—a resident of the District of Columbia.* His state-by-state analysis shows that the nine largest (California, New York, Pennsylvania, Texas, Illinois, Ohio, Michigan, New Jersey, and Florida) have a disproportionately large voting power.

Later in this chapter, we will see how the rules of the electoral college affect the campaign strategies adopted by presidential candidates. However, as indicated in the following section, there are other considerations that affect the nature of the presidential campaign.

THE PRESIDENTIAL CAMPAIGN

A presidential campaign involves the candidate and those working in the campaign in activities designed to motivate citizens to take the time and effort to vote, and to vote for *him or her*. However, voters' minds are not blank pieces of paper on which campaign activities are written. Instead, the average voter already has certain political attitudes and ways of looking at the political world that have been previously acquired. The key to securing an individual's vote, then, is to trigger somehow that person's political dispositions to result in a decision to vote for the candidate in question. As Dan Nimmo (1970: 5) suggests, ". . . Campaigns cause people to sort out their preferences, thus deciding which of the opposing camps to align themselves with on election day."

---

*One reason why Washington, D.C., voters are particularly disadvantaged in the electoral college is that under the provisions of the Twenty-third Amendment, the District is entitled to no more electoral votes than those of the least populous state. If it were treated as a state, the District would receive four electoral votes instead of the present three.

All presidential contests require candidates and their supporters to make a series of basic decisions affecting the conduct of the campaign. The first involves *the kinds of political appeals* that will be used to try to gain votes. The second is the means that will be used to *communicate* those appeals to the electorate. The third concerns the *targeting* of the campaign to best affect the outcome of the presidential contest. Finally, there are considerations involved in the overall *management* of the campaign. This means determining how basic resources, including people and money, can be acquired and used to obtain votes and how the entire campaign operation can be conducted to achieve maximum results.

Manipulating Political Appeals

Candidate Image. Because so much public attention in a presidential campaign focuses on the candidates themselves, the personality and character that the aspirants project are particularly important. Each campaign organization strives to create a composite *image* of the most attractive attributes of its candidate. Although the image necessarily deviates from reality, it must still reflect enough of the essential characteristics of the candidate to be believable. One effective tactic is to take a potential flaw and convert it into an asset. Thus, the elderly Dwight Eisenhower (he was 66 at the time of his second campaign in 1956) was pictured as a benevolent "father" (or even "grandfather") whose mature judgment was needed to lead the nation in times of stress. In contrast, the youthful John Kennedy (he was 43 when he ran for the presidency in 1960) was characterized as a man of "vigor" who would make America "feel young again" after the Eisenhower years.

Presidential candidates frequently take their opponents' images into account when shaping their own. In 1964 Lyndon Johnson represented himself as the candidate of moderation, thereby hoping to suggest that Senator Goldwater was an extremist. Gerald Ford portrayed himself as a man of maturity and experience to counteract Carter's emphasis on being a "new face" and an "outsider" to the Washington scene. Besides molding their own images to take account of their opponents', candidates can directly attack opposition candidates to put them in a bad light with the voters. Accordingly, Gerald Ford described Jimmy Carter: "He wavers, he wanders, he wiggles, he waffles" and charged that his opponent had a strange way of changing his accent: "In California he tried to sound like Cesar Chavez; in Chicago, like Mayor Daley; in New York, like Ralph Nader; in Washington, like George Meany; then he comes to the farm belt and he becomes a little old peanut farmer." During the second debate, after Ford claimed that Eastern Europe was not under Soviet domination, Carter countered that the president must have been "brainwashed" when he went to Poland. Carter was thereby comparing Ford with George Romney, the former Michigan governor whose nomination campaign collapsed in 1968 after he said he had been "brainwashed" by the military in the course of a trip to Vietnam. The Georgian also said that during the second debate Ford had "showed very vividly the absence of good judgment, good sense, and knowledge" expected of a president.

Not all candidates, however, think it is politically wise to attack an opponent. For example, Franklin Roosevelt thought that doing so only gave that person free publicity. Moreover, there is always the chance that voters will resent such tactics or that they may open the way to counterattacks. A classic case occurred in the presidential campaign of 1884. Republicans, seeking to take advantage of the accusation that the Democratic candidate, Grover Cleveland, had fathered a child out of wedlock (an accusation Cleveland never denied), composed the campaign ditty, "Ma! Ma! Where's my Pa? Gone to the White House, Ha! Ha! Ha!" The Democrats responded with a slogan that sought to remind voters of the charges of political dishonesty directed against the Republican candidate, James G. Blaine: "James G. Blaine, the continental liar from the state of Maine." Thus the voters that year were presented with a dilemma. Should they favor Cleveland, whose private life was morally questionable but whose honesty in public life had never been challenged, or should they vote for Blaine, whose family relationships were idyllic but whose conduct in public office made him seem risky? One of Cleveland's supporters offered a solution: "We should elect Mr. Cleveland to the public office which he is so admirably qualified to fill, and remand Mr. Blaine to the private life which he is so eminently fitted to adorn."

Generally, however, candidates spend more time trying to project a favorable image of themselves than casting aspersions on their opponents. In 1968 Nixon focused his attention on refurbishing his former portrait as a humorless and overly aggressive political infighter. In touching up the picture, he strove to present a "new Nixon" who could laugh at himself (referring to his 1960 loss to Kennedy and his performance in the presidential debates that year, he acknowledged being "an electoral college 'drop-out' who had flunked debating") and who had matured and become more humane over the eight years since he had last run for the presidency.

Party Label. Candidates deal with their party label in different ways. Considering the Democrats' status as majority party since the days of Franklin Roosevelt, it is not surprising that their candidates generally play up party affiliation and that their opponents do not. Therefore, in 1960, John Kennedy stressed that he stood "where Woodrow Wilson stood, and Franklin Roosevelt stood, and Harry Truman stood," whereas "his opponent stood with McKinley, Taft, Harding, Landon, and Dewey." In contrast, Nixon urged voters to ignore party labels and to vote for the "best man," the man with experience in foreign affairs who had stood up to Khrushchev and bested him in the kitchen debate in Moscow.

In 1976 Jimmy Carter opened his campaign in Warm Springs, Georgia, in order to associate himself with Franklin Roosevelt (who had visited there many times seeking comfort for his paralytic condition and where he died in 1945). Gerald Ford invoked no past Republican presidents (not even Dwight Eisenhower). Instead, he tied his candidacy to that of a former Democratic chief executive, Harry Truman who, as an underdog incumbent, struggled successfully for the same goal as Ford's: election to the office in his own right, not merely by succession.

At times, presidential candidates of both the majority and minority parties make a clear bid for the support of persons normally associated with the political opposition. In his quest to win an overwhelming victory over Barry Goldwater in 1964, Lyndon Johnson stated that he had "always been the kind of Democrat who could and would work together with my fellow Americans for the party of Lincoln and McKinley, Herbert Hoover and Dwight Eisenhower, Robert Taft, Arthur Vandenberg, and Everett Dirksen." In 1972 Richard Nixon, who also sought to win a landslide victory over Democratic candidate, George McGovern, charged that the Democratic convention had rejected many of the principles of that party and implored, "To those millions who have been driven out of their home in the Democratic party, we say come home."

As indicated in Chapter 2, whether or not candidates represent the majority or the minority party, prominent political figures in each party must support their campaigns if they are to be successful. In 1964 Goldwater's candidacy suffered (although it is unlikely that he could have won the presidency anyway), because some leading Republicans (including Governors Nelson Rockefeller of New York and George Romney of Michigan) dissociated themselves from the Goldwater-Miller ticket.

Incumbency. Incumbent presidents who are running for reelection start out with certain advantages in the electoral contest. They are typically better known to the voters than their opponents, who must strive to narrow the recognition gap between the two candidates. The incumbent president frequently assumes the role of statesman, too busy with the affairs of the nation to participate in a demeaning, partisan campaign. As Timothy Crouse (1972: 257) describes the 1972 campaign, "Around the White House, it bordered on treason to call Nixon a candidate." In 1976 Gerald Ford followed his advisors' recommendation by conducting the early stages of the campaign from the White House "Rose Garden," gathering presidential publicity by receiving visitors, signing or vetoing bills, and calling press conferences to make announcements.

While the incumbent president is playing the role of statesman operating above the partisan fray, others are free to make political attacks on the opposition. Frequently, the vice-presidential candidates assume that role, as Hubert Humphrey did for the Democrats in 1964 and Robert Dole did for the Republicans in 1976. Or the president's supporters may develop an entire team to carry on the effort. In 1972 the Committee to Reelect the President (note that Nixon's name did not even appear in the title of the committee) organized a special "surrogate's office" to schedule campaign appearances of thirty-five White House aides, cabinet members, senators, representatives, mayors, and Republican party officials.

Incumbent presidents have other advantages that are not available to challengers. For example, they may use their powers as chief executive to ensure that funds are used to develop governmental installations and projects in various states, or they may raise price supports, as Nixon did in 1972 on dairy products. Presidents may also schedule dramatic events to focus attention on their position as the nation's representative in international affairs. During 1972 President Nixon visited Communist China and the Soviet Union, gathering extensive media coverage in the process.

Of course, an incumbent president cannot control events entirely and in some cases, unfavorable ones can harm the chances of reelection. The Great Depression was the major reason for Herbert Hoover's defeat by Franklin Roosevelt in 1932, and the Watergate scandals, even though they were associated with his predecessor, Richard Nixon, undoubtedly contributed to Gerald Ford's loss in 1976.

However, even if things are not going as well in the country as would be hoped, an incumbent president can blame the Congress if it is currently controlled by the opposition party. In the 1948 campaign Harry Truman used the "do-nothing" Republican 80th Congress as a "whipping boy." In 1976 Gerald Ford tried a similar tactic by branding the Democratic 94th Congress as a "spendthrift" body that was responsible for the nation's problems with inflation.

Social Groups. Fairly early in life, many Americans begin to think of themselves as members of individual ethnic, geographic, or religious groups. As they get older, they also begin to identify with groups associated with their occupations and to consider themselves as businesspeople or farmers or as members of labor unions. Sometimes people may relate politically to groups to which they do not belong. For example, a well-to-do white liberal who sympathizes with the underdog in society may favor programs that benefit poor blacks. Moreover, such reference groups can also be negative: a self-made businessperson may have an unfavorable image of labor unions or social welfare organizations.

Presidential candidates take these group attitudes into account in devising campaign appeals. Since the days of Franklin Roosevelt, the Democratic party has aimed its campaigns at certain groups thought to be particularly susceptible to its political overtures. Included have been Southerners, blacks, members of ethnic groups, organized labor, Catholics, Jews, intellectuals, and big-city "bosses" and their political supporters. (Hence the quip that the Democratic party has more wings than a boardinghouse chicken!) At the same time, the Democrats have usually tried to depict the Republicans as the party of "Big Business" and the rich.

Republican candidates have been less likely to use explicit group appeals in their presidential campaigns. In fact, Senator Goldwater conducted an antigroup campaign in 1964. The Republican candidate seemed to go out of his way to antagonize particular blocs, speaking against the Tennessee Valley Authority (TVA) in Knoxville; against Social Security financing in retirement communities like St. Petersburg, Florida; and against the "War on Poverty" in Charleston, West Virginia, near the heart of Appalachia. (In writing off such groups as "minorities," Goldwater ignored the fact that an aggregation of minorities makes up a majority.) In 1968 Richard Nixon tried a different approach, aiming his campaign at the "Forgotten Americans who did not break the law, but did pay taxes, go to work, school, church, and love their country." (He thus sought to associate the Democrats with negative reference groups such as welfare recipients, atheists, and war protestors.) However, in 1972, hoping to capitalize on George McGovern's unpopularity with many traditional Democratic groups, the Committee to Reelect the President turned out campaign buttons and bumper stickers for almost thirty nationalities, provided copy for ethnic newspapers and radio stations, and made special appeals to Catholics, Jews, blacks, and Mexican-Americans.

As John Kessel (1974: 116) suggests, one of the most difficult aspects of designing a campaign is for a candidate "to appeal to voters in a manner acceptable to groups already supporting him." A presidential candidate must be careful that appeals to certain groups do not alienate others. The classic case of this dilemma occurred in Nixon's 1960 campaign. Initially, he hoped to win a number of black votes (Ike had done well with blacks in 1952 and even better in 1956), and so he capitulated to New York Governor Nelson Rockefeller's demands for more liberal platform provisions on race relations. Early in the general election campaign, Nixon visited Atlanta, where he received what he termed "the most impressive demonstration he had seen in his fourteen years of campaigning." After that, Nixon vacillated between trying to win the black vote and appealing to white Southerners. When Martin Luther King, Jr., was jailed in Atlanta for refusing to leave a restaurant table, Nixon took no action. However, Kennedy made a quick decision to take a campaign aide's advice to telephone Mrs. King and express his concern. King's father, who before the incident had been a Nixon supporter, switched his support to Kennedy; many observers credited this move with giving Kennedy enough black votes in closely contested states such as Illinois to win the election. Eight years later Nixon used a different tactic; he made a concerted effort to appeal to white Southerners and did not approach the black community at all. In contrast, Hubert Humphrey appealed to blacks and made no overtures to white Southerners.

Issues and Political Events. Although presidential candidates talk a lot about discussing the issues, they seldom do so in much detail. (In 1968 the *New York Post* remarked testily, "Mr. Nixon has published a collection of positions he has taken on 167 issues. It seems a pity he could not have made it a round 170 by adding Vietnam, the cities, and civil rights.") The candidates usually do focus on major problems in American society, but only in very general terms. A catchy slogan is often used by the out party to link the one in power with unfortunate political events; thus the "Korea, corruption, and communism" brand was stamped on the Democrats by Republicans in 1952. The party in power responds in the same way, as when the Democrats defended their record that same year by telling the voters, "You never had it so good." In 1976 the situation was reversed; Democrats talked about Watergate, inflation, unemployment, and President Ford's pardon of Richard Nixon (Carter refused to attack Ford on the issue, but his vice-presidential candidate, Walter Mondale, did), whereas President Ford claimed that his administration had cut inflation in half, brought peace ("Not a single American is fighting or dying") to the nation, and restored faith, confidence, and trust in the presidency.

This sort of general attack and defense characterizes most presidential campaigns. The party out of power has the advantage of associating all the ills of American life with the administration; the party in power is in the position of claiming that all of the nation's blessings have resulted from its leadership. The candidate who is in the most difficult situation is the nonincumbent nominee of the party in power, such as Nixon in 1960 and Humphrey in 1968. Both served as vice president in administrations whose policies they did not fully endorse. Nixon, for instance, did not believe Eisenhower was doing enough in space exploration and national defense. Humphrey opposed the bombing of North Vietnam when it was first initiated in 1965. Yet each hesitated to criticize an administration in which he had served. Humphrey's inability to disassociate himself from the Johnson administration's approach to Vietnam is considered one of the major reasons for his defeat in 1968.

Not only are issues usually framed in general terms in presidential campaigns but few concrete suggestions are made for handling them.* Thus, in 1960, Kennedy urged that he be given the chance to "get the nation moving again," but he was very vague about what, specifically, he would do to move the nation forward. Nixon was even more indefinite in 1968; he refused to spell out his plans for dealing with the major American political issue, Vietnam. His excuse was that if he did so, he might jeopardize the Paris peace talks that were then being held.

The 1972 McGovern campaign was a major exception to the pattern just discussed. It focused more on issues than former campaigns had, and the candidate made more specific suggestions for dealing with those issues. McGovern proposed that the defense budget be cut by 30 percent, and early in his campaign, advocated that all persons (regardless of need) be given a $1000 grant by the government.

In manipulating political appeals, candidates usually attempt to develop a *general theme* that will incorporate a wide variety of matters and leave the voters with an overall impression of the campaign. Sometimes the theme focuses on the

---

*Donald Stokes (1966: 170–171) calls "position issues" those that "involve advocacy of governmental action from a set of alternatives..." as contrasted to "valence issues," which "merely involve linking of the parties with some condition that is positively or negatively valued by the electorate."

candidates themselves, as did Humphrey's slogan, "He's a man you can trust." Or it may be essentially an appeal to a broad group, such as Nixon's "Forgotten Americans," who did not break the law but did pay their taxes, go to work, school, and church, and love their country. At other times, the theme is directed at issues and political events ("Korea, corruption, and communism" or "peace and prosperity"), or takes the form of Kennedy's general call for action, "We've got to get the nation moving again"; McGovern's plea, "Come home, America"; or Carter's promise to make the government as "truthful, capable, and filled with love as the American people." Once the theme is established, candidates try, by constant repetition, to get the electorate to respond emotionally to it. Their success in doing so, however, depends on another important aspect of presidential campaigns: how political appeals are communicated to the American voter.

Communicating with the Public

Considering our nation's large size and its population of more than 200 million, presidential campaigns must be carried to the American people primarily through the mass media.* Included are the two broadcast media, television and radio, and the print media, newspapers and magazines. Of these, television is by far the most important. Since 1952 it has been the chief source of campaign information for most Americans. Television's importance is intensified because it takes less effort to watch than it does to read, particularly since viewing can be combined with other activities, but reading cannot (McLuhan, 1964: Chap. 1). In addition, people are more inclined to believe what they see on television than what they read in the newspapers or hear on the radio. The illusion of being on the spot (many persons are not aware of the possibilities for staging a scene or event) helps create the feeling of political reality.

Presidential candidates have employed a number of television formats. Richard Nixon's 1968 campaign used short, sixty-second spot announcements during popular programs such as Rowan and Martin's "Laugh-in" and appearances before panels of citizens who asked questions that Nixon could answer in a seemingly spontaneous fashion. The makeup of both the panels and the questions were carefully screened by Nixon's advisers in order to avoid possible embarrassment or surprise. To make the show even more interesting, former football coach and television personality, Bud Wilkinson, intercepted the questions and lateraled them on to the candidate.

In 1972 the use of television for political communication underwent additional change. Although spot commercials continued to be used (one, for example, sym-

---

*Even Richard Nixon's herculean 1960 campaign, during which he gave speeches in 188 cities where some 10 million Americans saw him in person (White, 1961: 380), reached only about 6 percent of the then population of 180 million.

bolized McGovern's proposed cuts in defense spending by a hand sweeping away toy soldiers and miniature ships and planes), five-minute commercial advertisements became more common. There were also longer programs, consisting of a series of addresses by McGovern on Vietnam and the issue of corruption. Semidocumentary formats such as a candidate's discussing issues with the "man in the street" were used, as well. McGovern was filmed interacting with workers and small businessmen, and Nixon's trips to China and the Soviet Union were dramatized for television viewers.

In 1976 Ford utilized the medium somewhat more imaginatively than Carter. The president held an informal television interview with sportscaster and former baseball player Joe Garagiola, who tossed him some "gopher-ball" questions: "How many foreign leaders have you met with, Mr. President?", to which Ford modestly replied, "One hundred and twenty-four, Joe." In the last stages of the campaign, the Ford forces also broadcast short television interviews with voters in Georgia, who described Carter as "wishy-washy." Carter's use of television concentrated on short commercials in which he looked directly into the camera and talked about various issues, aimed at counteracting Ford's version of him and representing himself as a strong, positive leader with specific programs.

Of course, the use of television in presidential campaigns extends beyond what the candidates themselves develop and pay for. The major networks (NBC, CBS, and ABC) give extensive coverage to the campaign and devote substantial portions of their regular evening news shows to the activities of the candidates. In addition, in 1960 and again in 1976, debates between the two major party candidates (also included in 1976 was an exchange between the vice-presidential contenders, Robert Dole and Walter Mondale) were aired through arrangements with the three major networks.* Both presidential debates were considered major features of the two campaigns; Kennedy and Carter said after the campaign that they did not think they would have won the presidency if the debates had not been held. Moreover, Barry Jagoda, Carter's television adviser, saw the 1976 debates as a "surrogate campaign," and Sander Vanocur, television columnist for the *Washington Post,* viewed the campaign as "intermissions between those moments when Ford and Carter perform their three acts."

Despite the dominance of television in recent presidential campaigns, the other media continue to play a part in presidential campaigns. Radio is less expensive to use than television and can be utilized in ways that television cannot, such as broadcasting to commuting drivers, as Ford did in a series of early-morning chats during the 1976 campaign. There is also the distinct possibility that a particular

---

*A problem in holding presidential debates is a provision of the Federal Communications Act of 1934 requiring the networks to provide "equal time" to *all* candidates, including those of minor parties. In 1960 Congress temporarily suspended the provisions of the Act to allow the Nixon-Kennedy debates. In 1976 the debates were sponsored and paid for by the League of Women Voters. The networks supposedly covered them as "news events," a legal fiction that was exposed when the first debate was interrupted for twenty-eight minutes until an audio failure could be repaired.

candidate will come over better on radio, a reason suggested for Nixon's using that medium for more speeches than he delivered over television during the 1972 campaign.* Moreover, as with television, the radio networks devote a considerable amount of attention to presidential campaigns. In some cases, as with National Public Radio, the campaigns are carried in much more depth than on television.

Newspapers and magazines are another source of communication in presidential campaigns. Advertisements offer the potential for visual effects. In 1960 the Democrats used pictures of their handsome candidate and his attractive wife Jackie in many of their ads. In 1976 the Republicans printed full-page ads comparing a cover of *Newsweek* magazine, which featured President Ford, with the cover of *Playboy* magazine, that presented its controversial interview with Carter in which he confessed that he "lusted after women in his heart." Newspapers and magazines also comment extensively on presidential campaigns and, unlike television and radio networks, typically favor one candidate over another through endorsements made during the course of the campaign. Over the years those endorsements have clearly favored the Republican presidential candidate, except in 1964, when the press favored Johnson over Goldwater.

The formats available in the various media therefore make it possible to emphasize different types of political appeals and to reach disparate audiences. Based on their analyses of the 1972 presidential campaign, Patterson and McClure (1976) argue that television evening news programs concentrate on campaign "hoopla," how the contenders are faring in the "horserace," and convey almost no information on where the candidates stand on the issues. Radio and newspaper coverage of the campaign is much more effective in conveying the latter kind of information, as are five-minute commercial messages paid for by each candidate and party. They also contend that the longer (thirty minute) political broadcasts "attract only the highly partisan and have become the television equivalent of the traditional political rally" (p. 121). Nimmo (1970: 117–118) also distinguishes between two major types of audiences: first, the politically concerned and interested who use the print media as well as television and radio to obtain information on the presidential campaign; and the less politically involved person who must be reached through television and, sometimes, through radio, particularly by means of spot announcements such as those Richard Nixon used during his 1968 campaign.

Targeting the Campaign

The mass media, especially television, enable presidential candidates to make political appeals nationally, but candidates still plan a series of nationwide personal appearances during the campaign. For one thing, it is hoped that voters who come to

*One piece of evidence on this point is that those who heard the first Nixon-Kennedy debate in 1960 on the radio believed that the two candidates came out about equally; those who watched it on television thought Nixon did poorly compared to Kennedy (White, 1961: 348.)

see and hear a candidate in person may be inclined to vote for him as a result of this contact. (This assumption is questionable, since many persons turn out as a result of curiosity to see what a presidential candidate looks like, and may end up voting for his opponent.) In addition, there are other by-products of candidates' visits. Voters who do not attend the rally may be flattered that the candidate took the time to come to their area; moreover, local media will give special publicity to the candidate and potentially influence their special audience. Holding a rally in a populous metropolitan area with television and radio stations and newspapers that serve an entire state or several states is a promising strategy for presidential aspirants.

As previously mentioned, the rules of the electoral college affect the campaign strategies of presidential candidates. The goal is clear: to win the presidency one must win a majority of the total 538 electoral votes, or 270 votes. This fact places a premium on carrying those states with the largest number of electoral votes. The eleven largest states—California, New York, Pennsylvania, Texas, Illinois, Ohio, Michigan, New Jersey, Florida, North Carolina, and Indiana—together have a total of 271 votes, enough to elect candidates even if they lose the other thirty-nine states. Naturally, candidates from both major political parties tend to concentrate on these states as prime targets for personal visits.

Another element that affects candidates' decisions on where to campaign is the *competitive situation* in a particular state; that is, does the state generally go to one party's presidential candidate or does it swing back and forth from one election to the next? Distinctly one-party states are likely to be slighted by both candidates; the party in control does not think it necessary to waste time there (in 1968, Nixon did not visit or spend money in Kansas; as one campaign aide put it, "If you have to worry about Kansas, you don't have a campaign anyway"); in contrast, the opposition party is liable to think it futile to exert much effort on such obviously enemy territory.* (The only time the Democrats have carried Kansas in recent years was in the Johnson landslide in 1964.) The swing states—including the large ones just listed, most of which are politically competitive—draw the major portion of attention from presidential candidates of both parties.

Recently, each of the parties has developed areas where its presidential candidates are generally successful. The Republicans have been strongest in the West, and Democratic strength has been concentrated in the Northeast. The Midwest has been a competitive area that has attracted both groups. The situation in the once-solid Democratic South has varied with individual elections. It was vital in the electoral strategies of Kennedy in 1960 and Carter in 1976, and helped to put both men in the White House. On the other hand, Humphrey in 1968, and McGovern in 1972 wrote off the region, and the results reflected this decision. Humphrey carried

---

*Presidential candidates sometimes deliberately venture into states thought to belong politically to their opponents. Carter's plan in 1976 included visits into normally Republican areas in order to put Ford on the defensive and to make him spend time and money in states he would normally carry (Schram, 1977: 247).

only Texas (considered by some political observers to be a Western instead of a truly Southern state), and McGovern did not win in any of them.*

The most systematic plan in targeting a presidential campaign was developed for Jimmy Carter in 1976 by Hamilton Jordan. He assigned points to each state using three criteria. The first was the number of electoral votes. The second was its Democratic potential based on how many Democratic officeholders there were, along with how well McGovern had done there in 1972. The third was how much of a campaign was needed in a particular state, taking into account factors such as how well Carter had done in the preconvention period, how much time or resources he had previously expended in the state, and how close to Ford he was in the polls. The various campaigners were allocated points (for example, one day of Carter's time was worth seven points, Mondale's, five points, and a Carter child, one point) and then assigned to states so that scheduling points were matched with those developed under the political-importance formula.†

Thus, a presidential campaign involves a complex combination of political appeals, communicated by the media to voters residing in various regions of the country. As suggested in the next section, the overall management of the campaign becomes a major problem for the person who seeks the nation's highest political office.

Managing a Presidential Campaign

As the candidates and their staffs lay their plans for the presidential campaign, they face a series of key decisions. Should candidates emphasize their own qualifications and approach to public problems, or should they attack their opponent's programs? Should they agree to a debate? Is it best to emphasize their party label, or will that antagonize independent voters? Should they discuss issues and, if so, which ones should be singled out for attention? Which social and economic groups offer the best potential support for the candidacy, and how should they appeal to them? How much of the campaign budget should go to television, compared to newspaper advertisements or radio broadcasts? Which states should be especially targeted for campaign efforts, and which particular campaigners should be sent?

Such decisions are difficult, and they must often be made when the candidate and his staff lack enough information on which to base a judgment. At the time that Gerald Ford extended the challenge to debate to Jimmy Carter, the decision made a

*John Kessel (1974: 109) reports the comment made during the 1972 campaign that "McGovern could not carry the South with Robert E. Lee as his running mate and Bear Bryant as his campaign manager."

†This carefully thought out plan is to be contrasted with the pledge Richard Nixon made at the 1960 Republican National Convention to visit all fifty states personally. In the closing days of the campaign Nixon took precious time to fly to Alaska, which he had not previously visited, while his opponent, John Kennedy, was barnstorming through heavily populated Illinois, New Jersey, New York, and the New England states.

lot of sense. He was far behind in the polls and needed to do something to close that gap. Moreover, his training as a lawyer and long service as a member, and later minority leader, of the House of Representatives contributed to his debating skills. His experience as president also provided him with unique information and insights into national problems, especially in the field of foreign and military affairs. On the other hand, Carter, trained as an engineer, was not known for his talents as a speaker and debater, and his government experience was confined to one term as governor of a medium-size state.

In the first debate, Ford managed to best his hesitant and deferential opponent and, despite high unemployment and inflation, create the impression that he was a competent manager of the domestic economy. His success seemed to support the wisdom of his challenge to debate, particularly when Carter's lead in the polls thereafter continued to fall. However, the second debate, dealing with foreign and military affairs (in which Ford was supposedly advantaged by his incumbency and by the peacemaking efforts and successful diplomatic ventures of Henry Kissinger in Asia, the Middle East, and Africa), resulted in a victory for the inexperienced Carter and in the president's being embarrassed by his own unfortunate remark about eastern Europe's not being under Soviet domination. Pollster George Gallup reported that the second debate stalled Ford's momentum and enabled his Democratic challenger to regain some of his earlier popularity with the electorate.

Because it is difficult to foresee contingencies and because so much information must be gathered and so many activities coordinated, many political campaigns are not unlike some military battles where participants seem to wander aimlessly in all directions at once. The overall management of campaigns demands leaders with superb administrative skills who can put together and utilize information on diverse matters such as voting patterns in past elections, public attitudes on issues, and the best format for a television presentation.

Traditionally, political campaigns in the United States have been devised by candidates, their personal advisers, and party leaders on the basis of intuitive judgments and experiences in successful past contests. However, beginning in the 1930s in California, *public-relations firms* that had developed advertising programs for private businesses began to transfer their propaganda skills to persuading the public to vote for certain political candidates or for propositions put to the voters in referendums. Both parties have used professional firms and consultants of this type since the 1952 presidential election.

As indicated in Chapter 2, which dealt with nomination campaigns, these firms and consultants provide a variety of services for a presidential candidate. For example, they take public opinion polls inquiring into voters' attitudes on issues as well as their reactions to candidates and their opponents.* They research past voting

*At times the results can be devastating. By mid-October 1964 the Goldwater organization had canceled the polls taken by the Opinion Research Corporation because they did not want to "pay for tidings of disaster." (White, 1965: 396). During the 1972 campaign, Pat Caddell, the pollster for the

patterns and political preferences of various social, economic, and geographical groups. They also write speeches, plan press conferences, and oversee the use of the mass media. Together with the top staff members of the campaign organization, these firms and consultants plan and manage the overall campaign.

As David Leuthold (1968: Chap. 1) suggests, a political campaign is a process in which a candidate and his assistants acquire resources and use them to secure votes. Two such resources are particularly important in conducting the campaign. One is the organization of people who carry the campaign to the voters. The other is the money to pay for the entire cost of the campaign.

People: Campaign Workers. Although the mass media play a major role in communicating political appeals to the voters, interpersonal contacts remain an important instrument in shaping people's political decisions. Not everyone personally follows the presidential campaign in the media, particularly the parts that appear in print and on the radio. They are dependent on those who do follow it to pass on information on matters such as the presidential candidates' stands on the issues. (Of course, the transmitters often alter the messages in keeping with their own views and biases.) Beyond that, personal contacts are particularly important in getting many people to make the most basic political decision: whether or not to vote at all. Sometimes the only thing that will overcome the apathy of citizens is the dogged determination of someone to see to it that they get themselves registered to vote and then take them to the polls.

Presidential candidates typically start the general election campaign with a core of individuals who are close to them and who, in effect, constitute their personal organization. For an incumbent president, these people frequently come from his own administration. In 1964, Lyndon Johnson used three close aides, Bill Moyers, Jack Valenti, and Walter Jenkins, as key organizers in his presidential campaign in 1972. Originally, Richard Nixon put John Mitchell, his attorney general, in charge of the Committee to Reelect the President and transferred other persons in the White House office to assignments on the committee. For presidential candidates of the party-out-of power, the organizers assembled to help them win the nomination normally shift their attention to the general election phase of the presidential contest. Thus, John Kennedy put his brother Robert in charge of his 1960 campaign against Richard Nixon, and Hamilton Jordan continued as the head of Jimmy Carter's general election campaign. Along with the top aides, persons who worked out in the field during the primary campaign are also generally available for similar activities in the fall contest.*

McGovern organization, said that when he brought his results to campaign headquarters, he "felt like the recreation director on the Titanic" (White, 1973: 429).

*The importance of these primary campaign workers is illustrated by the situation in 1968. Since Humphrey won the Democratic nomination that year without entering a single primary, he had no such pool of workers available for his fall campaign.

Because the electorate for the general campaign is so much broader than the selectorate that participates in the nomination phase of the presidential contest, candidates must expand their fall supporters to include people who were not involved in their previous nomination campaigns.

One potential source of new recruits is political rivals, who may have sought the nomination themselves. In 1972 George McGovern asked Hubert Humphrey to campaign for him; Humphrey did so out of personal friendship and party loyalty.* Candidates may seek to co-opt not only the personal support of their rivals, but also that of their organizations of campaign workers. Moore and Fraser reported (1977: 133) that in 1976, in many states, the Ford and Reagan people cochaired the general election campaign. However, in many instances, personal loyalties and commitments to issues are so strong that it is not possible to recruit such workers. In 1968, the Humphrey organization was unsuccessful in getting many of Eugene McCarthy's supporters to work in the general election campaign after McCarthy lost the presidential nomination.

Persons associated with the regular party organization are another potential source of campaign workers. Termed "organizational loyalists" by John Kessel (1968: 179), these are the individuals who owe their allegiance to the party instead of to a particular presidential candidate or set of political issues. Because of such loyalties, they are often willing to work in the fall campaign for whichever candidate wins their party's nomination, no matter what their personal feelings about that person may be. At the same time, because they are pragmatic and not ideological, party loyalists may not work hard for a presidential candidate who they think is a loser and who will hurt the party ticket. Many Republicans took this attitude toward Goldwater in 1964, as did some Democratic leaders toward Humphrey in 1968 and McGovern in 1972. In addition, some state and local party leaders are more interested in races at that level because they are more important to the leaders' interests (particularly in patronage positions) than the presidency. Moreover, traditional party organizations have been declining for many years (the political machine of Chicago's late mayor, Richard Daley, is the major exception). Therefore, such organizations have a limited effect in presidential campaigns even when they are enthusiastic about their candidates and consider the election vital to their own interests.

Without powerful party organizations, recent presidential candidates have turned to other means to get out the vote. Lately, organized labor has helped to carry out that vital function, chiefly to the benefit of the Democrats. In 1968, working through its Committee on Political Education,† the AFL-CIO claimed to have

---

*Humphrey previously assisted McGovern greatly in his political career. Moreover, in 1968 McGovern had worked in Humphrey's campaign after he unsuccessfully sought the presidential nomination himself following the assassination of Robert Kennedy.

†Labor unions, like corporations, are forbidden by federal law to contribute money to either the

registered 4.6 million voters, printed and distributed over 100 million pamphlets, operated telephone banks in 638 localities, sent out 70,000 house-to-house canvassers, and provided almost 100,000 volunteers on election day to get people to the polls (White, 1965: 453–454). Of course, this effort was extended on Hubert Humphrey's behalf and is credited with eventually helping to swing into line a number of workers who initially planned to vote for George Wallace.

In contrast, the antipathy of George Meany and other AFL-CIO leaders toward George McGovern caused the organization to remain neutral in the 1972 presidential race, concentrating its efforts on helping to elect Democratic congressmen and state and local officials. In 1976 the AFL-CIO returned to its traditional policy of supporting Democratic presidential candidates and played an important role in getting its members and their families registered and to the polls to vote for Jimmy Carter on Election Day.

Another form of political organization that has become prominent in recent years is the *ad hoc committee* for a particular presidential ticket. Typically designated along the lines of "Citizens for Johnson-Humphrey" (sometimes the presidential candidate's name alone is used; sometimes it is not used at all, as in 1972 with the Committee to Reelect the President), they are designed to attract the support of persons who may not be willing to work with the traditional party organizations. They may appeal to people who consider political parties outdated or meaningless, but who favor particular candidates because of their personal magnetism or their stand on the issues. Ad hoc committees may also be valuable in winning the support of political independents or of people who generally support the opposite party. In some instances, separate organizations are formed to appeal to this latter group. This was done in 1972, when the Republicans created "Democrats for Nixon" under the leadership of Governor John Connally and then used the unit effectively to run commercials depicting the Democratic candidate, George McGovern, facing in opposite directions on political issues (May and Fraser, 1973: 199).

A well-run presidential campaign should be able to draw on all these sources of campaign workers. However, wounds sustained in the nomination campaign are sometimes difficult to heal by the time of the fall contest. Moreover, some of the groups regard each other with mutual disdain. The "Citizens for" types often think of regular party workers as political hacks who are in politics for their own materialistic interests and who will support any party candidate, no matter what his personality, character, or stand on issues. In turn, the party worker often regards the citizens' group workers as "station wagon" types who come out of the political woodwork every four years to campaign for a particular candidate, but who show no

---

nomination or the election of the president, vice president, or a member of Congress. The Committee on Political Education (COPE) was created as a separate organization to which union members can contribute voluntarily (union dues may not be used) for political activities.

concern for the long-range prospects of the party and no loyalty to it as an institution. Squabbles among local, state, and national party organizations are also common, since each feels that election races at its particular level are most important.
Rivalries have also traditionally developed among such groups over the allocation of
campaign donations and expenditures. However, as indicated in the following section, changes have recently been made in the financing of presidential campaigns
that have relieved this situation.

Money: Campaign Finances. As David Adamany (1972: Chap. 1) suggests, money
is a valuable political resource because of its *convertibility* and *transferability*. By
convertibility he means that it can be exchanged or turned into other resources such
as media time or space, or the building of an organization to do the grass roots work
of politics. By transferability he means that it can more easily be allocated to the
locale where politicians want it than can most other resources. With these advantages, it is understandable why Jesse Unruh, a veteran California politician, refers to
money as the "mother's milk of politics."

One of the major problems presidential candidates have faced in recent years is
raising enough money to mount an effective campaign. As indicated by Table 3.1,
after remaining stable during the 1940s, the costs of presidential general elections
rose in the 1950s and again in the 1960s. There was another dramatic increase
registered in the 1972 presidential contest. Table 3.1 also shows that Republican
presidential campaigns are generally more expensive than Democratic ones; the
single exception is the 1948 election, in which Truman outspent Dewey. Recently,
the disparity in party expenditures has become greater, with Republicans outspend-
ing Democrats by a two-to-one margin in the 1964, 1968, and 1972 elections.

A number of factors have contributed to this rapid increase in presidential
campaign costs.* One has been the growth in the use of mass media, particularly
television and radio. In 1968 the two major-party candidates together expended $19
million of the total $37 million spent in the general election that year on the two
media. Added to this figure, which includes only network and station charges, are
production and promotion costs, which sometimes run as high as 50 percent of the
media charge (Alexander, 1976: 29). Also contributing to the burgeoning of campaign moneys are the fees paid to political consultants for specialized services such
as conducting polls, raising funds, and preparing direct mail appeals. Thus the
increasing professionalization of presidential campaigns has brought with it spiral-
ing costs.

As with presidential nominations, general election campaigns have traditionally been financed by certain standard sources. One is *business*. Although

---

*Two of the more obvious ones are the size of the electorate and the cost of living in the United
States. However, campaign costs have risen faster than those factors, with the comparative increase
being most pronounced after the 1964 election.

Table 3.1 Costs of Presidential General Elections, 1940–1972

Year	Republican		Democratic	
1940	$ 3,451,310	Wilkie	$ 2,783,654	F. Roosevelt[a]
1944	2,828,652	Dewey	2,169,077	F. Roosevelt[a]
1948	2,127,296	Dewey	2,736,334	Truman[a]
1952	6,608,623	Eisenhower[a]	5,032,926	Stevenson
1956	7,778,702	Eisenhower[a]	5,106,651	Stevenson
1960	10,128,000	Nixon	9,797,000	Kennedy[a]
1964	16,026,000	Goldwater	8,757,000	Johnson[a]
1968	25,402,000	Nixon[a]	11,594,000	Humphrey
1972	61,400,000	Nixon[a]	30,000,000	McGovern

Source. Excerpted from Herbert E. Alexander, *Financing Politics: Money, Elections and Political Reform* (Washington, D.C.: Congressional Quarterly Press, 1976), Table 2.1, p. 28.
[a]Indicates winner.

they are legally forbidden to contribute directly to presidential campaigns, corporations have developed means of assisting candidates (most corporate money has gone to Republicans). These have included paying salary bonuses to officers with the understanding that they will make a personal contribution to a presidential candidate, contributions in kind (furniture, office equipment, and mailing lists), and payments to persons handling the corporations' public relations work that can easily find their way into electoral channels (Heard, 1960: 116). Similarly barred from contributing to presidential campaigns, *labor unions* have also devised methods of assisting presidential candidates (primarily Democrats). This is usually done through voluntary contributions from union members, expenditures to inform them about the candidates and to get out the vote, and public service activities, such as media programs that may have a partisan slant (Heard, 1960: 156–157). Both parties have also received gifts from wealthy individuals. In 1968 W. Clement Stone, chairman of the Combined Insurance Company of America, gave $2.8 million to Richard Nixon's campaign; four years later, Stewart R. Mott, heir to a General Motors' fortune, donated $400,000 to George McGovern's bid for the presidency.

Both parties have lately developed ways of expanding their source of moneys for presidential campaigns to include the small contributor. The Republicans in 1964 and the Democrats in 1968 benefited from a new solicitation technique. At the end of campaign television programs, viewers were asked to send in donations, which they promptly did to a much greater extent than had been anticipated. In 1972 both parties were highly successful in raising small contributions (under $500) by direct mail: estimates indicate that at least 500,000 persons contributed more than $13 million to the Nixon campaign, and 530,000 donated $15 million to the McGovern campaign. Since 1972, the Democrats have also used telethons—

nonstop telecasts hosted by show business celebrities and local volunteers—to raise donations, although the money has generally been used to pay off debts from past campaigns instead of for current or future ones.

After ignoring for decades major problems associated with campaign financing—the identity of persons and groups contributing to candidates, the possibility of favored treatment for large contributors, and the uneven distribution of resources between political parties and individual candidates—a wave of reform swept the country in the 1970s. In 1971 Congress passed the Federal Election Campaign Act; this act requires presidential candidates to file reports with the comptroller general *disclosing* detailed information on the money they raised and spent, including the names of all persons who contributed more than $100, and the nature of all expenditures of that amount or more. The same legislation also placed *restrictions* on the amount of money candidates and their families could contribute to their own campaigns ($50,000) and *limitations* on advertising in the media. In addition, the Revenue Act of 1971 encouraged small contributions by providing *tax credits* ($12.50) or *deductions* ($50) for political contributions and provided for the establishment of future *government subsidies* of major presidential candidates (those receiving 25 percent or more of the previous election vote), to be funded by $1 check offs on federal income tax returns.

However, the 1971 legislation had a limited effect on the 1972 presidential campaign. The public subsidy provisions of the Revenue Act were not yet applicable, and the Campaign Act did not take effect until April 7, 1972, which resulted in a rush to collect funds before that date. It is estimated that the Committee to Reelect the President (that is, Nixon) raised as much as $20 million prior to April 7. In addition, the committee raised large cash contributions from persons who did not want their identity known (many were traditional Democrats who did not like McGovern) and then sought to conceal their sources in a variety of ways, including transmitting funds through banks in Mexico. Several executives of major corporations pleaded guilty to making illegal contributions to the presidential race, suggesting that the money was, in effect, extorted from them under pain of losing certain financial advantages they enjoyed from the federal government if they refused to contribute. Allegations were also made that representatives of the dairy industry made large donations to the Nixon campaign in return for an increase in government support of milk prices. Finally, disclosures showed that moneys collected were used to finance "dirty tricks" against leading Democratic candidates, such as Senator Edmund Muskie in the nomination campaign, and to provide funds for people involved in the Watergate burglary. Thus, ironically, the first presidential election conducted in the new era of election reform ranks as the most scandalous in American history.

Reacting to the 1972 campaign abuses in October 1974 after President Nixon had resigned, the Congress passed and President Ford reluctantly signed into law legislation amending the 1971 Federal Election Campaign Act. The previous restrictions on contributions by candidates themselves and their families were retained and new ones were added. A limit of $1000 for individuals and $5000 for committees was set for each primary or general election. In addition, a $1000 limit was placed on independent expenditures made on behalf of a candidate, and cash contributions of over $100 and those from foreign sources were barred altogether. Previous limitations on media spending were repealed and were replaced by overall limits on presidential primary and general election expenditures. Particularly significant was the provision of partial public funding for presidential primaries (as we saw in Chapter 2, matching funds up to $5.5 million were granted to any candidate successful in raising a total of $5000 in each of twenty states in individual amounts of $250 or less) along with full public funding of the costs of the general election. Finally, the 1974 legislation provided for full disclosure of campaign contributions and expenditures (including those by persons making independent expenditures on behalf of a candidate), and also created a full-time, bipartisan Federal Election Commission composed of six members (two each appointed by the president, speaker of the house, and the president *pro tempore* of the Senate) to administer the federal election laws and public finance program.

The battle over campaign finances, however, was soon moved to the courts. On January 1, 1975, a number of individuals and groups, including New York Senator James Buckley (a conservative), former Minnesota Senator Eugene McCarthy (a liberal), members of the Conservative Party of the State of New York, and the New York Civil Liberties Union, filed a case in the federal courts challenging the constitutionality of the campaign finance legislation. The case was eventually appealed to the Supreme Court and, on January 30, 1976, the Court handed down an historic decision in *Buckley* v. *Valeo*. Faced with balancing the two rights of free speech involved in the use of money to communicate political appeals, and the rights of Congress to protect the integrity of federal elections, the Court declared certain provisions of the legislation unconstitutional at the same time they upheld others. The Court concluded that limitations on the amount of expenditures by candidates and their families, and by individuals making independent expenditures on behalf of a candidate, together with overall limits on campaign expenditures, were direct and substantial restraints on political speech and, hence, were unconstitutional. (However, the Court qualified its ruling on these matters by holding that, although independent spending on behalf of candidates could not be limited, it was illegal to coordinate such spending with the candidates' or their campaign organizations, and that if candidates accepted public financing—which the Court sustained—they would have to accept the limitations on overall expenditures as a condition of the grant.)

On the other hand, the Court sustained the restrictions on the amount of contributions by individuals and political committees on the grounds that they made only a marginal restriction on the contributor's ability to engage in political communication. The justices also upheld the disclosure provisions of the campaign finance law and the concept of a bipartisan commission to administer it. However, the Court ruled that as long as the commission was within the executive branch of government, the separation of powers principle required that all its members be appointed by the president. The court granted the Congress thirty days to restaff the commission.

This last ruling forced Congress to act again on campaign finance. The legislation, however, was interrupted by a new controversy—the role that corporations, labor unions, and membership organizations (such as trade associations) should be able to play in political campaigns—and failed to meet the thirty-day deadline imposed by the Supreme Court for reconstituting the Federal Election Commission. The Court extended the period another twenty days, but Congress also missed that deadline. As a result, the commission lost its authority to provide matching funds after March 22, 1976. It did not regain that authority until two months later, in late May, when the legislation was eventually passed and President Ford chose the six new members of the commission. In the meantime, however, Congress resolved the controversy noted above by establishing a $5000 limitation on contributions by political action committees of corporations, labor unions, and membership organizations to a candidate in a single campaign. It also stated that expenditures made by such groups in excess of $2000 per election, which involve communications advocating the election or defeat of a clearly identified candidate, must be reported to the Federal Election Commission. In addition, the 1976 legislation required individuals and political committees making an independent political expenditure of more than $100 for the defeat or election of a candidate to report the expenditure and to state that it was not made in collusion with a candidate.

Campaign finance legislation and the *Buckley* v. *Valeo* decision had some effect on the 1976 presidential nomination race. As we saw previously, thirteen Democratic candidates, plus President Ford and Ronald Reagan were able to qualify for federal matching funds. This subsidy probably allowed some of them to remain in the race longer than would have been the case if they had had to depend on private donations alone.* The two-month delay in the availability of federal matching funds did not seem to have been harmful to the leading candidates. President Ford's and Jimmy Carter's finances were in fairly good shape at the time of the cutoff in funds, and Ronald Reagan was able to borrow money until the federal funds to which he was entitled became available again.

The recent legislation and judicial actions on campaign finance had a much greater effect on the 1976 fall election campaign. Both Ford and Carter decided to accept the public funds ($21.8 million each) and were therefore restricted to that figure (plus another $3.2 million that each national committee could spend on behalf of its presidential candidate) for the entire campaign. This meant that the Republi-

*One of the 1976 amendments, however, provides that in the future, such funds will be cut off to a candidate who wins less than 10 percent of the vote in two consecutive presidential primaries.

cans had to forego their traditional advantage in campaign funds. Moreover, both sides had to conduct more restricted campaigns than they did in 1972, when the Republicans spent $61 million and the Democrats $30 million. Both campaigns devoted about half their total moneys to television and other media advertising, which meant that they had limited funds available for organizing the campaign at the grass roots level. Buttons, bumper stickers, and yard signs, which were used extensively in former campaigns, were missing, as were the fund-raising activities of former elections. Campaign organizations were even forced to turn down "in-kind" (as contrasted to cash) donations such as hot-air balloons, sound trucks, and Coke machines for fear that they would violate legal restrictions against coordinating outside activities with those of the candidate's own organization. As a result, there was less spontaneity in the 1976 presidential campaign, a situation that some observers felt affected voter turnout at the polls. We will examine this latter topic in Chapter 4.

CHAPTER 4

Voting in Presidential Elections

The major purpose of presidential campaigns is to motivate persons to take the time and effort to vote, and to vote for a particular candidate. However, other factors also determine whether certain voters will cast a ballot in a presidential election. Moreover, for those who vote, the ultimate choice they make between candidates depends on their long-term political predispositions, such as political-party loyalties and social-group affiliations. Their choice also reflects their reactions to short-term forces such as particular candidates and issues involved in specific elections.

PARTICIPATION IN PRESIDENTIAL ELECTIONS

As previously indicated, the Founders originally intended that the process of choosing the president and vice president would be restricted to members of the electoral college, the political elite of the day who were thought to have the intelligence and information to choose the best people to lead the country. The average person was considered incapable of making decisions of this kind. However, such assumptions were soon nullified by important developments in American politics. As a result of the formation of the rival Federalist and Republican parties in the 1790s, electors began to vote the presidential preferences of the electorate instead of exercising their own judgment. Moreover, state legislatures that were granted power by the Constitution to determine how the electors should be chosen soon began vesting that right in the general electorate. In the process, our presidential election system changed from an "elitist" to a "democratic" one.

This development was highly significant, but it left an important question unanswered. Who should be entitled to vote for the presidential electors? To make matters even more uncertain, under our Constitution, that decision was left to the individual states, so that it was possible for some states to allow certain persons to vote for president while others prevented them from doing so. As a result, it has sometimes been necessary for the federal government to take action to force all states to allow certain groups of persons to participate in the selection of the chief executive.

An early state barrier to participation in presidential elections was *property ownership*. Many legislatures took the position that such ownership was necessary in order to give individuals enough of a "stake" in society to interest themselves in its political affairs. Some legislators were also concerned that the poor would sell their votes to unscrupulous politicians or, worse, use their votes to choose candidates who would proceed to redistribute the wealth of property owners. However, as more and more persons acquired property and redistribution of wealth failed to materialize, state legislatures began to drop the property qualification for voting in presidential and other elections. By the early 1840s such qualifications had generally disappeared at the state level. Thus the first major expansion of the presidential electorate took place without federal intervention, a situation to be contrasted with other battles over the composition of the presidential electorate.

The most bitter franchise struggle involved the right of *blacks* to vote in all elections, including presidential contests. At the end of the Civil War, as part of a concerted program to bring liberated slaves into the mainstream of American life, the Fifteenth Amendment was passed. It prohibited the United States or any state from denying any citizen the right to vote on account of "race, color, or previous condition of servitude." For a short time, blacks did participate in presidential and other elections but, when federal troops withdrew from the South in the 1870s, a systematic disenfranchisement of blacks began. It took many forms, including the use of physical violence and economic coercion, and legal devices such as excluding blacks from participating in primaries of the dominant Democratic party, and requiring them to pay poll taxes,* and to pass literacy tests (which were unfairly administered by election officials) in order to vote.

Unlike the property tax voting qualifications that the states themselves eliminated, it has been necessary for the federal government to take action on many occasions to force states to extend the right to vote to blacks. The earliest pressure came from the federal courts. In a 1915 decision, *Guinn* v. *United States,* the Supreme Court invalidated the "grandfather" clause of the Oklahoma constitution,

---

*Such taxes also disenfranchised many poor whites in the South.

which exempted persons from a literacy test if their ancestors were entitled to vote in 1866; the Court viewed this as a deliberate (and not too subtle) attempt to avoid the Fifteenth Amendment's prohibition against denying citizens the right to vote on account of "race, color, or previous condition of servitude." Ultimately, the Court also outlawed "white" primaries, ruling in *Smith* v. *Allright* (1944) that such an election was a *public* function (and not the business of a private organization, the Democratic party, as had been held in 1935), and hence was forbidden by that amendment.

The other two branches of the national government lagged behind the courts in helping blacks to win the right to vote. Democratic Presidents Franklin Roosevelt and Harry Truman both favored their enfranchisement, but they were unsuccessful in persuading a Congress dominated by Southern committee chairmen and possessed of the filibuster power to block legislation to move against poll taxes or even to enact an antilynching law. It was not until 1957, during the Republican administration of Dwight Eisenhower, that Congress finally passed legislation giving the attorney general of the United States the right to seek judicial relief against persons violating the right of individuals to vote. However, that law was easily circumvented by many Southern election officials who continued to harass blacks who tried to vote and who also destroyed records to cover up their actions. Three years later Congress passed additional legislation that strengthened the enforcement of voting rights by authorizing courts to appoint voting referees to register persons deprived of the right to vote on account of race or color and making it a crime to destroy federal election records.

Building on these moderate beginnings, in the 1960s Congress launched an attack against the disenfranchisement of blacks. It initiated the Twenty-Fourth Amendment outlawing the use of the poll tax in presidential and congressional elections;* that amendment was ratified by the states in early 1964. The following year, Congress responded to President Lyndon Johnson's leadership by enacting the Voting Rights Act of 1965, which suspended literacy tests and authorized the appointment of federal examiners to supervise electoral procedures in areas using such tests where less than one-half the voting-age population was registered or voted in 1964. The act was subsequently amended in 1970 to cover areas where a similar situation existed in November 1968. In 1975 the act was extended for seven years more and its provisions were expanded to cover the voting rights of other minorities, including persons of Spanish heritage, American Indians, Asian-Americans and Alaskan natives.

The national government has also taken action to expand the electorate to include two other major groups: *women* and *young people*. Even though some states had acted on their own to enfranchise both groups, Congress ultimately decided to

---

*In a 1966 decision, *Harper* v. *Virginia,* the Supreme Court eliminated the payment of a poll tax as a requirement for voting in state elections by ruling that it violated the equal protection clause of the Fourteenth Amendment.

require all states to do so. In 1920 the states ratified the Nineteenth Amendment, which forbade either the United States or any state from denying any citizen of the United States the right to vote on account of sex. Young people won a major victory in the early 1970s. Congress first passed a law granting eighteen-year-olds the right to vote in national, state, and local elections. When the Supreme Court ruled that a national law could affect only voting in national elections; the Twenty-Sixth Amendment was enacted to extend the right to state and local elections.

Congress has recently initiated two other actions to expand the presidential electorate. The Twenty-Third Amendment grants residents of the District of Columbia the right to vote in presidential elections, a privilege they had been denied since the capital was located there at the beginning of the nineteenth century. The 1970 act that lowered the voting age to eighteen also provides that persons are entitled to vote in presidential elections if they have lived at their current residence for at least thirty days.

Thus the number of people who are eligible to vote in presidential elections has increased greatly over the years. However, as the following sections indicate, the right to vote and the actual exercise of that right are two separate matters.

General Trends in Voting Turnout

One of the ironies of American presidential elections is that as more and more citizens have acquired the right to vote in recent years, there has been a trend toward a smaller and smaller proportion of them exercising that right. As Table 4.1 indicates, the estimated number of persons of voting age has almost doubled since Franklin Roosevelt was first elected to office in 1932. However, after reaching a peak in 1960, the percentage of people who actually went to the polls has declined in the last four presidential elections. The most pronounced drop—over 5 percent—occurred between the 1968 and 1972 elections.

This recent decline in voter participation runs counter to some of the traditional theories that attempt to explain why people do not vote. Frequently, restrictive laws, particularly those relating to registration and voting, are said to prevent citizens from going to the polls. Yet many states have eased such restrictions in recent years and, as just mentioned, the Congress has facilitated voting in presidential elections for new residents, so that it was generally easier for a person to register and vote for a president in 1976 than in 1960. Nonvoting is also often attributed to a person's lack of education; however, the level of education of American citizens was higher in 1976 than in 1960. The failure to vote is frequently linked to a lack of political information. However, because of increased use of the mass media, and particularly because of the televising of the Ford-Carter debates in 1976, more Americans than ever (an average of 87 million tuned in on the three debates) were made aware of the candidates and their views on public issues. Finally, close political races are supposed to stimulate people to get out and vote because they think their ballot might

Table 4.1   Participation in Presidential Elections, 1932–1976

Year	Estimated Population of Voting Age (Millions)	Number of Votes Cast (Millions)	Percentage of Vote Cast
1932	75.8	39.7	52.4
1936	80.2	45.6	56.9
1940	84.7	49.9	58.9
1944	85.7	48.0	56.0
1948	95.6	48.8	51.1
1952	99.9	61.6	61.6
1956	104.5	62.0	59.3
1960	109.7	68.8	62.8
1964	114.1	70.6	61.9
1968	120.3	73.2	60.9
1972[a]	140.1	77.7	55.5
1976[a]	150.0	81.6	54.4

Source. Statistical Abstract of the United States, 1977, Table No. 813.
[a]Elections in which persons eighteen to twenty years old were eligible to vote in all states.

conceivably make a difference in the outcome. All the pollsters correctly forecast that the 1964 and 1972 elections would be landslides and the 1968 and 1976 elections cliff hangers, but a smaller percentage of persons voted in 1968 than in 1964, and participation also declined between 1972 and 1976.

It is possible to attribute some of the decline in voter turnout in recent years to the extension of the right to vote to eighteen-year olds, which first took effect in the 1972 presidential election. Analyses of participation in that election by age group (see Table 4.2) show that eighteen to twenty-year olds did not vote as much (proportionately to their number) as did persons twenty-one and over. Therefore, some of the overall 5 percent decline in voter turnout between 1968 and 1972 was caused by the addition of persons to the potential electorate in the latter year who were less inclined to vote. However, this factor does not help to explain the decline in participation between 1964 and 1968 and again between 1972 and 1976. Moreover, analyses of the 1972 election indicate that persons twenty-one and over did not participate as much proportionately as they did in 1968 (see Table 4.2).

The precise reasons for the decline in voting in recent years are not known for certain, but it does seem that more and more people are making a deliberate decision not to cast their ballots. Some, particularly those with limited education and interest in politics, continue to fail to vote because of *indifference,* but they are being joined by other, better-educated individuals who are concerned with political matters but who do not vote because of *cynicism* and *mistrust of politicians.* A 1976 national study of a group of nonvoters (defined as those of voting age who had voted in two or fewer previous elections, who had not registered that year, or who said that their chances of voting in the 1976 presidential election were 50 percent or less) by Peter D. Hart Research Associates, Inc., of Washington, D.C., indicated that the main reasons why such persons said they did not vote were that "candidates say one thing and do another," and that, "it doesn't make any difference who is elected, because things never seem to work out right." The same study also indicated that among persons who did not intend to vote that year were a number of "political dropouts," individuals who had cast their ballots frequently in the past, particularly during and prior to the 1968 election. Reasons for nonvoting also pointed to lack of political leadership: 62 percent of the dropouts said they would vote if the political system

Table 4.2   Voting Participation of Various Groups (by Percentage)[a] in Presidential Elections of 1968, 1972, 1976

	Year		
Group Characteristic	*1968*	*1972*	*1976*
Male	69.8	64.1	59.6
Female	66.0	62.0	58.8
White	69.1	64.5	60.9
Black	57.6	52.1	48.7
18–20 years old	—	48.3	38.0
21–24 years old	51.1	50.7	45.6
25–34 years old	62.5	59.7	55.4
35–44 years old	70.8	66.3	63.3
45–64 years old	74.9	70.8	68.7
65 and over	65.8	63.5	62.2
Residence			
Metropolitan	68.0	64.3	59.2
Nonmetropolitan	67.3	59.4	59.1
North and west	71.0	66.4	61.2
South	60.1	55.4	54.9
School year completed			
Grade 8 or less	54.5	47.4	44.1
Grade 9 to 12	61.3	52.0	47.2
Grade 12	72.5	65.4	59.4
More than 12	81.2	78.8	73.5

Source. The Statistical Abstract of the United States, 1977, Table 814.

[a]Based on estimated population of voting age.

could produce a candidate worth voting for. (Asked to name a politician who they most admired, 50 percent of the total nonvoters chose John Kennedy and 20 percent chose Franklin Roosevelt; in contrast, 1 percent chose Gerald Ford and Jimmy Carter.)

There has been a general decline in voting turnout in recent years, but the phenomenon is not universal. For example, every one of the twelve Southern states that Jimmy Carter carried had a greater percentage turnout in 1976 than it did in 1972, some evidence that regional pride was involved.

Group Differences in Voting Turnout

In Table 4.2, we saw that there are variations among groups as to their participation in presidential elections. One significant pattern revealed by the table is that several lower-participating groups—blacks, women, and young people—were formerly denied the franchise. One possible reason for this pattern is that some of the "newly" enfranchised may still be affected by public attitudes that originally denied them the right to vote. Thus, even after fifty years, some women (particularly those from the South who are older and less educated) cling to the belief that their place is in the home and that politics is none of their business. Similarly, nonwhites, especially older people who grew up in the South, may feel that they are not able to make good choices between candidates. In time those attitudes may change (as indicated by Table 4.2, in 1976 the traditional gap between male and female voting participation virtually disappeared), but there is a lag between the legal elimination of an impediment to voting and the removal of the attitudes and reasoning that underlie it.

Some group differences in voter turnout are rooted in psychological feelings that affect all kinds of political participation, including voting. Well-educated people are more likely to be aware of political developments and their significance than poorly-educated people. In addition, well-educated persons tend to feel politically efficacious. That is, they have a sense of confidence about the value of their opinions and believe that people in public office will listen to them; therefore, they think that what they do has an important effect on the political process. Poorly educated persons, however, are likely to feel that political officials do not care about them or their opinions. General attitudes about other persons also affect voting behavior; those who trust people are more likely to cast their ballots than those whose cynicism and hostility toward others make them feel politically alienated.

The influence of a group is frequently important. Thus, if individuals belong to a business organization or labor union whose members talk much about political affairs, they may develop their own interests in such matters. If so, their political interests will lead them to make the effort to vote. Moreover, even if people are not interested in politics, they may feel that it is nevertheless their duty as a citizen to vote. This attitude is much more likely to exist in the upper and middle classes than in the lower class.

If the reasons that prompt certain people to vote and influence others to remain at home on election day are varied, the factors that shape preferences between competing groups of presidential candidates are even more complex.

VOTING PREFERENCES IN PRESIDENTIAL ELECTIONS

The reasons underlying voting decisions have long been of interest to students of democratic politics. Some political philosophers created the model of the rational citizen, who carefully studies the major issues that society faces, decides what public policies are needed to deal with them, and chooses the candidate whose views on such matters are closest to his or her own. Viewed in this context, the results of elections turn on the "issues" and the candidates' stands on them. Historians, journalists, and other political observers writing on individual campaigns, have similarly focused on issues, along with dramatic events and personalities, as the key elements in election outcomes. They have also been inclined to attribute a victory or a defeat to campaign strategies.

Survey techniques developed in the United States in the 1930s made it possible to interview a carefully selected sample of persons on some matter and, on the basis of their responses, to generalize how a much larger group feels. These techniques became highly useful for eliciting the reasons behind electoral decisions. Instead of relying on what other persons *thought* the reasons were, it was now possible to get them from the voters themselves. Moreover, instead of focusing on what the voters *should* consider in making voting decisions, the emphasis now turned to what they actually *did* take into account.

In-depth studies of voters' attitudes began in the 1940 presidential campaign in Erie County, Ohio (Lazarsfeld, Berelson, and Gaudet, 1944); another study followed the 1948 campaign in Elmira, New York (Lazarsfeld, Berelson, and McPhee, 1954). These early studies, originally conducted to analyze the ways in which media coverage during the campaign changed voters' attitudes and behavior, instead demonstrated that voting behavior was more closely linked to long-term factors such as affiliation with social groups (churches, unions, political parties) and social class differences in income, occupation, and education. Thus, the major approach of these studies was *sociological:* they related voting behavior to group membership and social status.

Immediately after World War II, another group of specialists on consumer behavior at the Survey Research Center of the University of Michigan at Ann Arbor began to study voting in the 1948 presidential election. They did not concentrate on a single community, but interviewed a nationwide sample of Americans on how they voted in that election and why they voted as they did. Moreover, their general approach to voting was *psychological*, not *sociological*. Instead of emphasizing group affiliations and social status, the Michigan group emphasized the psychological motives, including *party identification,* attitude toward the *candidates,* and *issues* of a particular election, that prompted individuals to vote in a certain way.

The 1948 venture was a pioneering, experimental one but, beginning with the

1952 election, the Michigan group provided a comprehensive and systematic analysis of each presidential election. In 1960 four of the scholars at the Survey Research Center (Campbell, Converse, Miller, and Stokes) published a classical study, *The American Voter,* based on data gathered for the 1952 and 1956 elections. For many year, this study was the "bible" for students of voting behavior in the United States. Later, the Michigan group established the Inter-University Consortium on Political Research through which scholars from all over the United States and abroad share the election data gathered each four years. This arrangement has proven successful, because a number of studies analyzing presidential voting from 1952 to 1972 have been published. As we will see, these studies indicate that there has been a substantial change in the voting behavior of Americans over the two decades, particularly since the 1964 presidential election.

The following discussion focuses on the major factors that influence how persons vote in presidential elections. Included are voters' identifications with political parties and social groups and their reactions to issues and candidates associated with particular elections.

Party Identification

The Michigan group conceives of *party identification* as one of the key elements that affects how persons decide to vote in presidential elections. Its method of measuring that sense of party commitment is based on answers to certain questions in sample surveys. Voters are first asked whether they usually think of themselves as Republicans, Democrats, Independents, or what? Those identifying themselves as Republicans or Democrats are asked whether they would call themselves "strong" or "not very strong" members of either party. Those who say initially that they think of themselves as Independents are then asked whether they think of themselves as "closer" to the Republican or Democratic party. On the basis of their answers, respondents are placed in one of seven categories: Strong Republican, Weak Republican, Strong Democrat, Weak Democrat, Independent Republican, Independent Democrat, or Independent Independent.

As indicated in Table 4.3, the party identification of the American electorate was fairly constant from 1952 to 1964, which Philip Converse (1976: 34) refers to as the "steady state period." On the average, about three-quarters of the voters identified with one or the other of the major political parties; the remaining one-quarter thought of themselves as Independents. However, after the 1964 election, this second group began to increase—primarily at the expense of the Democrats—until it constituted one-third of the electorate in 1972. (It was also noteworthy that even those persons who stayed with the Democratic party were more inclined than before to say that they were "weak" rather than "strong" Democrats.) Moreover, after 1964, more people considered themselves Independents than identified with the Republican party. Thus voters' commitments to political parties as perceived by voters themselves have declined appreciably in recent years.

Table 4.3   Party Identification, 1952–1976 (Expressed in Percentages)[a]

	1952	1956	1960	1964	1968	1972	1976
Strong Democrat	22	21	21	26	20	15	15
Weak Democrat	25	23	25	25	25	25	25
Subtotal	47	44	46	51	45	40	40
Strong Republican	14	14	13	13	14	13	9
Weak Republican	13	15	14	11	10	10	14
Subtotal	27	29	27	24	24	23	23
Independent Democrat	10	7	8	9	10	11	12
Independent Republican	7	8	7	6	9	11	10
Independent Independent	5	9	8	8	11	13	14
Subtotal	22	24	23	23	30	35	36

Source. The University of Michigan Center for Political Studies.
[a]The percentages do not total 100 percent because of "don't know" responses.

Other students of voting in presidential elections have preferred to measure voters' commitments to, or independence of, political parties on the basis of their *behavior* instead of their self-perceptions and self-descriptions. V.O. Key (1966) analyzed the extent to which persons "switched" their vote from the candidate of one party to another between 1940 and 1960. DeVries and Tarrance (1972) focused their attention on what they termed "ticket-splitters," those who cast a ballot for candidates of more than one party for different offices in the same election. Both approaches show an increasing independence of parties. Key found from 1940 to 1960 that one-eighth to one-fifth of the electorate switched their votes from one presidential election to the next. The Michigan election data show that from 1968 to 1976 the proportion ranged from one-fifth to one-third. In 1952 some 13 percent of Americans voted a split ticket in presidential-Senate-House races; by 1972 that figure had risen to 30 percent.

Thus independence of political parties, either measured by voters' subjective attitudes toward the parties themselves or by reports of their decisions in the voting booth, has increased in the United States in recent years. However, as analyzed by Nie, Verba and Petrocik (1976: Chap. 4), this rise in political Independents is not spread evenly across the voting population. It has occurred primarily among young people, particularly those who entered the electorate in 1964 or later. As indicated by Figure 4.1, which traces cohorts of various-aged voters over the twenty-four year period, established voters (those who were twenty-five or older in 1952) have not become noticeably more Independent over the years. The percentage of increase is only 2 percent over the twenty-year period. The next two groups (new voters in

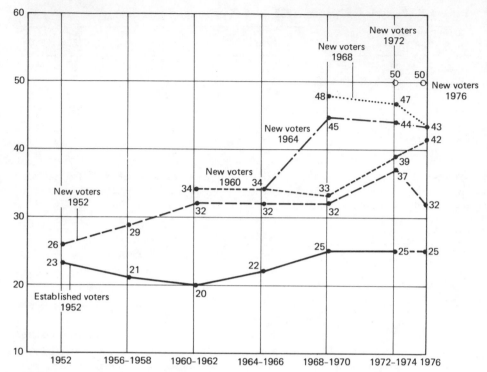

Figure 4.1. Proportion of Independents by age cohorts, 1952 to 1976. [*Source.* Norman Nie, Sidney Verba, and John Petrocik, *The Changing American Voter* (Cambridge, Mass.: Harvard University Press, 1976), p. 63. The 1976 figures are derived from data provided by the Inter-University Consortium on Political Research.]

1952 and 1960) were somewhat more Independent when they entered the electorate than the established 1952 voters, and they have also become more Independent over the years. However, new voters in 1964, 1968, and 1972 were most affected. The first group began with the same proportion of Independents as the 1960s cohort (34 percent) but then became considerably more Independent than the latter in 1968, while new 1968 and 1972 voters began with a high level of Independents.

The data in Figure 4.1 indicate that even though some increase in Independents in this country has occurred recently because individuals have abandoned their party home, most of it has been caused by the influx of new voters. The figure also shows that contrary to some assumptions, people do not necessarily become more partisan as they grow older. Only the established 1952 cohort declined significantly in proportion of Independents, and that by only a few percentage points for the time between 1952 and 1960. Thus partisan affiliation seems not to be related closely to *life cycle*—a particular chronological stage in an individual's life—but instead to *political generation,* the particular era when a person comes of political age.

Recent analyses of Independents in the United States indicate that they have grown dramatically in numbers and that they have also changed in character. Campbell et al. found that Independents in the 1950s were often less knowledgeable than party adherents about political issues and candidates and participated less in the political process. However, Pomper's analysis (1975: Chap. 2) of the behavior of Independents in recent elections indicated that they are just as knowledgeable about political matters as partisans. Although they are not as likely to vote as partisans, Independents do participate as much as, or even more than, partisans in other political activities, such as writing to political officials and voting in referendums. Thus nonpartisanship, rather than general political disinterest, characterizes many of the younger Independents, particularly those with a college education. What has happened is that a new type of Independent has been added to the ranks of the older kind that was prevalent in the 1950s.

A recent analysis by Miller and Miller (1977) also indicates that important differences exist among Independents who are contemporaries. Those who are "leaners," that is, feel closer to either the Republican or Democratic party, are usually younger, better educated, and in higher-status occupations than the independent Independents. Thus, the label "Independent," which has frequently been used to include leaners and true Independents, may obscure the partisan dispositions that exist among such groups.

It is difficult to determine the reasons for the decline in partisanship among American voters. One factor has been a lessening in the transfer of partisanship from one generation to another. As Nie, Verba, and Petrocik (1976: 70–72) point out, beginning in the late 1960s, younger voters became less likely to retain their family partisan affiliation than had occurred in the past. Converse (1976: Chap. 4) identifies two "shock" periods that weakened partisan loyalties. The first, beginning in 1965 and stemming from the Vietnamese conflict and racial unrest, affected persons of all ages, but Democrats somewhat more than Republicans. The second, starting in 1972, which Converse associates with the Watergate revelations and the disclosures that precipitated the resignation of Vice President Agnew, had a distinct impact on older Republicans. A change in the effect that social groups have on political attitudes has also contributed to the lessening of party commitments. We will discuss this topic in the next section.

Social Groups and Social Class

The early voting studies of presidential elections in the 1940s showed that a fairly close association existed between social group membership and social status on one hand, and support for one of the two major parties on the other. Democrats received most of their support from Southerners, blacks, Catholics, and persons with a limited education and income and a working-class background. Republican candidates were supported by Northerners, whites, Protestants, and persons with higher levels of education and income and a professional or business background.

Table 4.4 shows how various groups voted in presidential elections from 1952 through 1976. There was a general decline in the level of support that many of these groups gave their traditional party's candidates over the twenty-four-year period. Especially noticeable for the Republicans was their loss of votes from white-collar workers and Protestants. The most significant drop for the Democrats came from the Southern vote in the 1968 and 1972 elections. However, this vote was gained in 1976 by the Democratic candidate from Georgia, Jimmy Carter. The only group that significantly increased its support for its traditional party candidate over the twenty-four years was nonwhites, who were more firmly in the Democratic camp in 1976 than in 1952.

Table 4.4 also shows the effect that circumstances of particular elections can have on group voting. In 1964 all the groups—including those that typically support Republicans, such as the college-educated, professionals, and business people, along with Protestants and Westerners—voted for the Democratic candidate, Lyndon Johnson. In 1972 all the groups that traditionally sympathize with the Democrats, with the exception of nonwhites, voted for the Republican candidate, Richard Nixon.

Thus party identification and group affiliation have not meant as much in recent presidential voting as they once did. As the following sections indicate, short-term forces such as issues and candidates are now more important in the political world of the American voter.

Political Issues and Ideology

Campbell and his associates, who analyzed the voting behavior of Americans in the 1950s, suggested (Chap. 7) that issues are potentially important in determining how individuals cast their ballots only if three conditions are met. First, persons must be aware that an issue or a number of issues exist. Second, the issue or issues must be of some concern to them personally. Third, voters must perceive that one party better represents their own positions and thinking on the issue or issues than the other party.*

When the Michigan group applied these three conditions to the American voters in the 1956 presidential election, they found that relatively few voters met the three criteria. About one-third of the persons in their survey were not aware of *any* of the sixteen major issues about which they were questioned. Moreover, many of the two-thirds who were aware of one or more issues were not personally concerned about the matter. Finally, a number of those who were aware and concerned about issues were not able to perceive differences in the positions the two parties took on such issues. The result of the analysis was that at the most, only about one-third of

---

*Also included as a part of issue awareness was some notion of what the federal government was doing with respect to the matter.

Table 4.4 Vote by Groups in Presidential Elections Since 1952 (Based on Gallup Poll Survey Data)

	1952		1956		1960		1964		1968			1972		1976	
	Stev.	Ike	Stev.	Ike	JFK	Nixon	LBJ	Gold.	HHH	Nixon	Wallace	McG.	Nixon	Carter	Ford
	%	%	%	%	%	%	%	%	%	%	%	%	%	%	%
National	44.6	55.4	42.2	57.8	50.1	49.9	61.3	38.7	43.0	43.4	13.6	38	62	50	48
Race															
White	43	57	41	59	49	51	59	41	38	47	15	32	68	46	52
Non-white	79	21	61	39	68	32	94	6	85	12	3	87	13	85	15
Education															
College	34	66	31	69	39	61	52	48	37	54	9	37	63	42	55
High school	45	55	42	58	52	48	62	38	42	43	15	34	66	54	46
Grade school	52	48	50	50	55	45	66	34	52	33	15	49	51	58	41
Occupation															
Prof. & business	36	64	32	68	42	58	54	46	34	56	10	31	69	42	56
White collar	40	60	37	63	48	52	57	43	41	47	12	36	64	50	48
Manual	55	45	50	50	60	40	71	29	50	35	15	43	57	58	41
Religion															
Protestants	37	63	37	63	38	62	55	45	35	49	16	30	70	46	53
Catholics	56	44	51	49	78	22	76	24	59	33	8	48	52	57	42
Region															
East	45	55	40	60	53	47	68	32	50	43	7	42	58	51	47
Midwest	42	58	41	59	48	52	61	39	44	47	9	40	60	48	50
South	51	49	49	51	51	49	52	48	31	36	33	29	71	54	45
West	42	58	43	57	49	51	60	40	44	49	7	41	59	46	51
Members of labor union families	61	39	57	43	65	35	73	27	56	29	15	46	54	63	36

Source. Excerpted from *The Gallup Opinion Index* (December, 1976), pp. 16–17.

the electorate *potentially* voted on the basis of issues. (The proportion who *actually* voted as they did because of issues could have been, and probably was, even lower.)

More recent studies of political attitudes in the 1960s and early 1970s by Pomper (1975) and Nie, Verba, and Petrocik (1976) show a rise in the potential for voting on the basis of issues. There has been an increase in the number and kinds of issues that voters recognize. Although the Eisenhower years were characterized by some voter concern for traditional domestic issues (welfare, labor-management relationships) and foreign policy matters (the threat of international communism, the atomic bomb), beginning with the 1964 election, the scope of such concerns broadened to include new issues such as civil rights and Vietnam. Vietnam in particular continued to affect voters in the 1968 and 1972 contests and was joined by new matters such as crime, disorder, and juvenile delinquency. (These, along with race problems, were sometimes referred to collectively as "the social issue.")

Analyses of political attitudes in the 1960s and early 1970s indicate that persons were not only aware of more and varied issues, but that such issues had a greater impact on their lives. Studies by Cantril and Roll (1971: Chap. 1) show that in 1959, when Americans were asked about their hopes and fears for the future, they were most likely to refer to *personal* matters such as good or bad health, or the aspirations or problems of their children. Even though Americans were still concerned about these matters in 1964 and 1971, they were not as preoccupied with them. Many citizens began to think more about *political* issues (those requiring the intervention of government), such as world peace, inflation and, by 1971, drugs, pollution, and crime.

Finally, the connection between voters' own attitudes on issues and their perceptions of where the parties stand on the issues has recently grown closer. Gerald Pomper's analysis (1975: Chap. 8) of voters' attitudes on issues from 1956 through 1972 shows that beginning with the 1964 presidential election, attitudes became related to their partisan identification. Democrats were more likely to express the "liberal" position on economic, civil rights, and foreign policy issues than Republicans. Also, voters since 1964 better perceive than previous voters that differences exist between the general approach each party takes on such issues. Moreover, there has been an increasing consensus among such voters that Democrats take a liberal stance on the issues and Republicans a conservative one. These developments, coupled with the growth of voter awareness of political matters that are salient to them, means that the potential for voting on the basis of issues has increased in recent years. Correlations of voters' attitudes on issues with the way they voted in presidential elections also show that since 1964, this potential for issue voting has been converted into reality.

Contemporary analyses also indicate a change in the way the American people think about politics. When voters in the 1950s were asked by the Michigan group to indicate what they liked or disliked about the candidates and the parties, only about one in ten responded in ideological terms by linking attitudes on such matters to political issues or by utilizing concepts such as liberal or conservative to describe differences between candidates and parties. More people made references to *group benefits*—such as Democrats helping the "working class" and Republicans the "business people"—or to *the nature of the times,* linking Democrats to foreign wars and Republicans to economic downturns and depressions. Furthermore, over one-fifth of the voters in the 1950s gave replies that had no issue content at all, such as "I just like Democrats better than Republicans," or "Ike's my man." More recent studies by Nie, Verba, and Petrocik (1976: Chap. 7) have shown that the number of "ideologues" and "near-ideologues" has increased considerably, to about one-third of the electorate in 1964, 1968, and 1972. Particularly noticeable is a movement away from thinking about politics primarily from the perspective of group benefits and toward viewing it in broader terms of issues and general political ideas.

Another aspect of this broadening of the conceptualization of politics is voters' increased ability to be able to relate political issues to one another on the basis of a liberal-conservative dimension. Studies of the electorate in the 1950s by Philip Converse (1964) showed that voters displayed what he called a lack of "constraint"—that is, a low level of consistency—in attitudes on political issues. For example, persons who took the liberal position that government should take an active role in providing welfare for the needy did not necessarily think it should assume a similar role in encouraging racial integration in the schools; nor were voters' attitudes on either domestic matter related to their opinions on the foreign policy issue of what stand the government should take toward the threat of world communism. However, Figure 4.2, developed by Nie and Andersen (1974), indicates that beginning with the 1964 election and extending through the election in 1972, there was a higher correlation of attitudes on the various issues. Voters' positions on domestic issues were more likely to be consistent with one another as well as with their attitudes on foreign policy issues than previously.

Many persons assumed that the decline in social unrest growing out of the U.S. involvement in Vietnam and the racial tensions that gripped America in the late 1960s and early 1970s would mean a return to a less ideological and issue-related presidential election in 1976. However, Miller and Miller's analysis (1977) of that election indicates that this did not occur. Using the same criteria to discern the development of ideological thinking in the earlier period—liberal and conservative attitudes on issues possessed by voters, their perceptions of party differences on such matters, and a correlation between their attitudes on various issues—led Miller and Miller to conclude that there was only a slight decline in such thinking between 1972 and 1976. As far as issues were concerned, they found that economic matters were much more important to the electorate that latter year than social or cultural issues; Democrats were particularly concerned over the rise in unemployment prior to the election. The fact that many voters believed that the Democratic party would do a better job in dealing with unemployment than the Republican party would and the

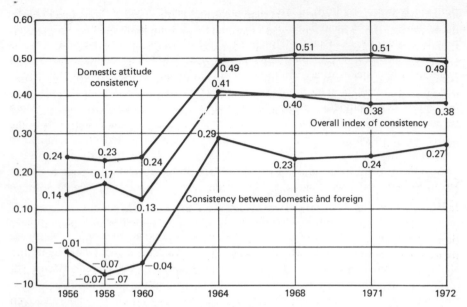

Figure 4.2. Changes in attitude consistency, 1956 to 1972. [*Source.* Norman Nie and Kristi Andersen, "Mass Belief Systems Revisited: Political Change and Attitude Structure," *The Journal of Politics, 36* (August 1974), Fig. 4, p. 558.]

fact that Carter placed particular emphasis on economic as compared to noneconomic issues in his campaign, prompted many voters to distinguish between the two parties and their respective candidates on that basis. The outcome that year was a much closer link between attitudes on economic issues and the voting decision than on social and cultural attitudes and how persons decided to cast their ballot in the presidential race.

Thus the interest of Americans in issues has increased in recent years, and voters are more likely than they once were to be able to relate issues on the general basis of liberalism and conservatism. These changes could conceivably be due to the rise in the educational level of the electorate between 1952 and 1976. However, although analyses do show that better-educated persons are more knowledgeable and concerned about issues than the less-educated persons, the greatest *increase* in knowledge and perceptions concerning issues over the twenty-four-year period still occurred among persons in the less well-educated group. What seems to be true is that the electorate's increasing sensitivity to political issues is not due primarily to alterations in the electorate itself, but instead to changes in the political environment in which elections have taken place from 1952 to 1976. Political events such as the war in Vietnam and the developments in race relations in the United States were more dramatic and salient to voters than the issues of the 1950s, which included the more abstract threat of international communism and the traditional economic conflict between labor and management. Moreover, presidential candidates such as Barry Goldwater and George McGovern took more definite stands on controversial issues than candidates in the Eisenhower years did; they also tended to tie issues together more closely in liberal and conservative packages than their predecessors did. The result of these developments was the sending of clearer signals to the electorate on where the respective parties and candidates stood on the vital issues of the 1960s and 1970s.

Candidates

Information on the influence of candidates on the outcome of elections is less reliable than is the part that parties and issues play in voting in presidential elections. As Warren Miller and Teresa Levitin (1976: 42) suggest, it is much easier to focus on the specific qualities of a particular candidate, such as Eisenhower's personal warmth, Kennedy's youth and Catholicsim, and Johnson's expansive style, than it is to compare candidates systematically over a series of elections.

Recognizing these limitations, it is nonetheless possible to make some overall comparisons of how voters reacted to candidates from 1952 to 1976. Each presidential year, the Michigan group asked people whether there was anything about each of the major candidates that would make them want to vote for or against that candidate. The total number of favorable and unfavorable comments can then be tabulated for each candidate; the more favorable (as compared to unfavorable) comments a candidate receives, the more positive the overall score is. The overall scores (positive and negative) of the two major party candidates can then be compared with one another to determine the relative appeal of the two candidates in any given election year. Figure 4.3 shows the appeal evoked by the different candidates from 1952 to 1976.

Two major findings are revealed by Figure 4.3. One is the variability in the reactions that voters demonstrated toward the candidates over the course of the seven presidential elections. The differences in candidate appeal were much less pronounced in 1952, 1960, and 1968 than they were in 1956, 1964, 1972, and 1976. The second finding is that except for two elections, 1964 and 1976, the Republican candidate was more favorably evaluated by voters than the Democratic candidate. Although it is not noteworthy that Dwight Eisenhower was more popular than Adlai Stevenson in 1956 and that Richard Nixon received a more favorable rating from the voters than George McGovern in 1972, it is somewhat surprising to find that Nixon was evaluated higher by the voters than John Kennedy in 1960.

It is difficult to determine why Republican candidates have generally been more popular lately than their Democratic opponents, but Herbert Asher (1976:

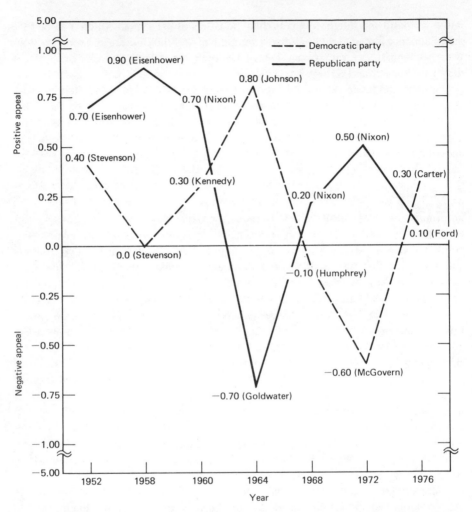

Figure 4.3. Appeal evoked by Democratic and Republican candidates for president, 1952 to 1976. [*Source.* Arthur Miller and Warren Miller (1977). "Partisanship and Performance: Rational Choice in the 1976 Presidential Election." Paper delivered at the annual meeting of the American Political Science Association, p. 10. (Data are from the American National Election Studies conducted by the Center for Political Studies, University of Michigan.)

Chap. 5) has suggested some possibilities. One is that the Democratic party draws support from a broader variety of divergent groups than the Republican party, and this makes it more difficult to please all elements of the Democratic party. Another possible explanation is that since Republicans are clearly the minority party, they have to be particularly concerned with nominating very attractive candidates. Finally, the nature of the times has favored Republican candidates. In 1952 and 1968 the incumbent Democratic party was faced with defending the Korean and Vietnam wars; such hostilities were either over or virtually over when the Republicans were the incumbent party in 1956 and 1972.

Voters' attitudes on candidates stem from numerous sources, including the associations they make between candidates and their partisan affiliations, their stands on issues, perceptions on how they have managed or would manage the government, and personal qualities such as background and experience, personality and character traits, personal and political "styles," and competence and trustworthiness. Miller and Miller's (1977) analyses of voters' reactions to the two presidential candidates in 1976 indicates that evaluations of President Ford were based primarily on his past performance in office and his trustworthiness. Carter was judged for the most part on the basis of his party identification and a partisan ideology that combined future expectations of which party and candidate would do a better job in the future, particularly in dealing with economic problems. As the authors stated, the results of the 1976 election ultimately turned on "incumbent performance versus partisan ideology" (p. 109).

Thus voting in presidential elections is influenced by many forces. Over the years, candidates of the two major parties have been associated with different sets of factors. Democrats have been favorably regarded for their party affiliation, their attitudes towards social groups, and their stands on domestic issues. In contrast, Republicans have benefited from their stance on foreign policy issues, their party philosophy, their perceived ability to manage the government, and a generally favorable assessment of them as candidates.

Campbell and his associates (1964: Chap. 16) have categorized presidential elections according to different clusters of electoral factors. An election in which the long-term partisan orientation of the electorate results in keeping the traditional majority party in power (since 1932, the Democrats) is a *maintaining election*. The majority-party candidate wins primarily because the voters make their choice on the basis of traditional party loyalties. Short-term forces such as candidates and issues are present but, instead of determining which party wins, they contribute to the size of the majority party's victory. When they favor that party, as they did in 1964 when the Goldwater candidacy benefited Democrats, the vote margin separating the two major candidates is larger than usual. If short-term forces are in balance, as they were in 1948, the vote division approximates the proportion of voters who generally identify with the two parties.

A *deviating election* occurs when short-term forces sufficiently benefit the minority party that they override the long-term partisan preferences of the electorate. An especially appealing candidate or an outstanding issue or event allows the minority party candidate to win with the support of some majority-party members, Independents, and a good share of new voters. The electorate does not, however, change its basic party preferences. Examples of deviating elections are those in 1952, 1956, 1968, and 1972: they were won by the Republican candidates, Eisenhower and Nixon, but the commitment of many persons to the majority party—the Democrats—was unaltered.*

An election that brings about major political change is referred to as a *realigning election*. Such elections involve a major realignment of electoral support among blocs of voters who switch their traditional party affiliation. An unusual number of new voters may also enter the electoral arena and cast their ballots disproportionately for one party's candidate. Unlike the deviating election, the effects of the realigning election persist in durable loyalties to the advantaged party. Political historians usually include five elections in the realigning category: 1800, 1828, 1860, 1896, and 1932.

Thus American presidential nominations and elections involve complicated rules, diverse candidate strategies, and difficult choices for the American people. Chapter 5 presents an overall assessment of our presidential contests.

---

*Analysts refer to an election following a deviating period as a *reinstating* one, because it reinstates the usual majority party in power. Examples are the 1960 and 1976 elections, when the Democrats returned to power after the two Eisenhower and the two Nixon victories. Thus a reinstating election is like a maintaining one in that long-term partisan factors determine the result.

5

Assessment of Presidential Contests

This chapter first summarizes the major changes that have occurred in presidential contests over the years and the factors that have contributed to those changes. In the second section of the chapter I give my own evaluation of the advantages and disadvantages of the current system, with particular attention to how well it meets the major functions served by elections in a democratic society. The final section analyzes proposals for improving our presidential contests and suggests those that offer the most promising prospects for effective reform. All three sections focus first on presidential nominations before discussing the general election.

MAJOR CHANGES IN PRESIDENTIAL CONTESTS

The dominant trend in American presidential contests has been one of *democratization* as, over the years, more and more persons have participated in the process of choosing our chief executive. Originally conceived by the Founders as a highly restrictive system in which members of the political elite from the various states would select the country's highest public official, within a decade the system underwent a radical change when rival political parties developed in the new nation. After that occurrence, the selection process was divided into two distinct parts: the nomination and election of the president. Moreover, after this separation took place, both phases of the selection process continued to change in the direction of participation by more and more people in both the nomination and election of the chief executive.

The nomination of the president has paralleled the development of our two major political parties. Both parties originally developed in the Congress, and so it was natural that they originally used legislative caucuses to nominate their presidential candidates. However, as the power base of the parties spread to state and local arenas, it became necessary to develop a nomination process that would include persons involved in political activities at those levels. At the same time, the process had to facilitate the choice of a candidate that would be acceptable to party activists in the diverse regions of the country. A national nominating convention comprised of delegates chosen by all the states emerged to meet these dual purposes of representation and unification.

The national nomination convention, first developed in the 1830s, is still the method that both major political parties use to choose their presidential nominees. However, the methods utilized to select the delegates to those conventions have undergone major changes over the years. Permitting party and public officials to choose delegates directly, or to influence their choice indirectly by dominating and manipulating local and state caucuses and conventions, has given way in recent years to methods designed to involve more rank-and-file citizens in the delegate selection process. Included are reforms regularizing the caucus-convention system and the enactment and revision of presidential primary laws by a number of states. The result of such changes, particularly those that have occurred in the 1970s, has been most dramatic. The numbers of persons participating in presidential primaries more than doubled between 1968 and 1976, rising from 12 million to 26 million over the eight years.

The presidential selectorate has broadened, and *political elites* who play an especially influential role in the choice of presidential nominees have also changed substantially. State party leaders, together with state and national public officials (governors, senators and U.S. House members), who used to control the state selection process and the national conventions, are no longer dominant figures in presidential nomination politics. The early endorsement of Edmund Muskie in the 1972 contest by a number of Democratic party and public officials did not prevent the party from ultimately choosing George McGovern, a candidate with whom many such professionals felt most uncomfortable. Four years later an "outsider," Jimmy Carter, won the Democratic nomination, even though he had virtually no initial support from any of his fellow governors or other members of the Democratic political "establishment." On the Republican side, Barry Goldwater won the 1964 Republican nomination despite the opposition of a number of party leaders and public officials. In 1976 Ronald Reagan came close to capturing the nomination from Gerald Ford, even though the incumbent president was supported by most Republican professional politicians.

Of growing importance are the political *amateurs* who have been active in both parties on behalf of candidates associated with specific issues or the general "antiestablishment" figures who have been dissatisfied with the "politics-as-usual" approach to the nation's problems. Dedicated to putting persons who will implement their own views of the "public interest" into the presidential office, amateurs reject party professionals' traditional criteria for presidential nominees: persons who will help compromise differences among the contending factions of the party and maximize its chances for victory in the November election. Instead, amateurs place a premium on picking candidates who stand for the "right" things and express the proper sentiments, regardless of whether or not they are likely to be electoral winners.

Another group that plays a role of growing importance in presidential nomination politics is the *media*. Under the former system, party professionals communicated directly with each other in deciding on the party's nominee; today the media are the vital link among the candidates themselves and between the candidates and the broadened selectorate. One of the nation's most distinguished and influential political reporters, David Broder (1973: 20–33), suggests that newspeople are now the principal source of information on what presidential candidates are saying and doing. In the process they undertake a variety of roles, including (1) acting as "talent scouts" to discover able presidential candidates; (2) summarizing the candidates' positions; (3) performing as race callers or handicappers by assessing the chances of victory of the various contenders; (4) acting as the "public defenders," in order to expose candidates who try to "dupe the voter," and (5) becoming volunteer, unpaid assistant managers for candidates. Thus journalists perform a variety of political roles in the campaign, many of which used to be the province of party and public officials.

Finally, *communication specialists* now play a major part in presidential nomination campaigns. Political organizations today include *public relations experts, media consultants, speech writers, direct-mail money raisers,* and *pollsters* who help the candidate carry the campaign to the general public. The services of such persons have professionalized presidential politics and have also driven up the costs of nomination campaigns.

Fortunately for many presidential aspirants, however, major changes have also occurred in the methods used to raise campaign funds. Dependent in the past on large contributions from party "fat cats" to finance their efforts, candidates in both parties have recently been successful in using the broadcast media and direct mail solicitations to gather money from small contributors. The new campaign finance law also encourages that approach by providing matching funds (up to a total of $5.5 million) for candidates who can raise a total of $5000 in each of twenty states in amounts of $250 or less.

Another major development in presidential nominations is the growing *nationalization of the process.* That trend is particularly evident in the development of new rules for choosing delegates to the national convention. Traditionally, both parties have permitted states to work out their own methods of selecting delegates, but that situation has changed drastically in recent years, especially in the Democratic party. A number of new rules developed by a series of party commissions and ultimately adopted by the Democratic National Committee and the National Convention now place major limitations on the operation of both the caucus-convention and presidential primary systems.*

Another indication of the nationalization of presidential nominations is the change in the political backgrounds of the persons chosen by both parties to represent them in the general election. Prior to the 1960s, it was customary for nominees to be "favorite sons" of their particular state; they often served as governor at the time of their selection. Since the 1950s, however, only one nominee, Adlai Stevenson, has used that particular route to the nomination.† Instead, recent nominees have been national political figures, coming from the Senate or the vice presidency to become their party's presidential candidate.

Finally, major changes have occurred in the *timing of the nomination campaign*. A reluctant candidate is no longer drafted by the national convention, as Adlai Stevenson was in 1952. Now presidential candidates, particularly those who are not well-known nationally, must begin their campaigns early. Also, they must enter and win a substantial number of presidential primaries and state caucus-convention contests in order to establish their claim to the nomination. Those who win receive the major share of publicity from the media and begin to raise their standings in the public opinion polls. As a result of this reinforcement process, the nomination decision is often actually made before the convention meets, and the body convenes to ratify the selection of the candidate who has captured the most delegate votes and who is the leader in the public opinion polls at the time. One demonstration of this change is that since World War II, only two candidates, Republican Thomas Dewey in 1948 and Democrat Adlai Stevenson in 1952, have not been nominated on the first ballot at the national convention.‡

Many of the changes that have taken place in the election of the president parallel those associated with the nomination process. Just as the presidential selectorate has broadened over the years, so has the electorate. Very early in the nation's history, state legislatures gave up their own right to choose the presidential electors and vested it in the general public. Since that time, more and more persons have become eligible to choose the presidential electors directly and the president indirectly. By the 1840s, most states had enfranchised individuals who did not own

---

*The Supreme Court has recently declared that national party rules are in most circumstances superior to state laws. The leading case on the subject is *Cousins* v. *Wigoda,* 419 U.S. 477, (1975).

†The last position that Jimmy Carter held prior to his being nominated for president was governor of Georgia, but he was not serving in that office at the time of his nomination.

‡As Leon Epstein (1978: 181–182) suggests, however, some first-ballot nominations do not simply register a clear preconvention consensus on the nominee. For example, although President Ford won the 1976 Republican nomination on the initial roll-call vote, the vote was very close and hardly consensual.

property. More recently, blacks, women, and young people have been added to the presidential electorate. Moreover, residency requirements have been eased in presidential elections, making it possible for more persons in our highly mobile population to cast their ballots on election day for the nation's chief executive.*

The nature of the campaign waged by candidates to win their party's nomination also carries over into the general election. Although party workers are available who may have worked for another presidential candidate or stayed out of the nomination contest altogether, for the most part nominees continue to rely on members of their personal political organization to provide overall management of the general election campaign. Such campaigners also employ the same kinds of specialists—public relations firms, media consultants and pollsters—that helped them win the presidential nomination in the first place.

The *media* also continue to play an important part in the general election. The candidates spend more of their own money on the media (especially television) than on any other component of the campaign, and the major networks and newspapers and magazines devote a great deal of time and effort from September to November to covering the campaign. Moreover, media commentators and facilities are a major feature of presidential debates, such as those that occurred in 1960 and 1976.

Moneys provided by the new campaign finance law have also affected the general election campaign. If anything, the total public funding of the campaigns (as compared with the matching funds available to those seeking their party's nomination) make candidates even more independent of party leaders and contributors than they are when they run for the presidential nomination. The new law provides some funds to be spent by the parties ($3.2 million), but that amount is much too small to mount an effective nationwide campaign. Moneys granted to presidential candidates themselves ($21.8 million), plus those available from political action committees and other contributions or expenditures independent of either the candidates or the parties, are crucial to the success of today's presidential campaigns.

The parties mean less today in terms of furnishing workers and money for the general election campaign, and they also provide a less significant clue to the electorate in choosing between the presidential candidates. More Americans have declared themselves to be political Independents lately and have switched their vote from one presidential election to the next as well as split their vote among party candidates running for different offices in the same election. Moreover, loyalties of particular social groups to the two parties have eroded. Republican candidates can no longer count as heavily as they used to on receiving the Protestant, middle-class, white-collar vote. Southerners, Catholics, Jews, members of various ethnic groups, and labor union members are no longer as solidly Democratic as they once were. Persons vote in presidential elections more and more on the basis of their reactions

*Note, however, that since 1960, the percentage of persons actually voting in presidential general elections has been declining, which differs from the situation in presidential nominations.

to the candidates themselves or to the major issues facing the country at the time of the contest, and not because of party or social group loyalties.

Several factors have contributed to the vast changes that have occurred in the nomination and election of the president. Some of the changes, particularly those associated with the nomination process, are a product of alterations made in the rules that were initiated to alter the former system of choosing the presidential nominees. As James Ceasar (1978: 736) has suggested, the Democratic reform commissions took the position that the old-style political organizations had lost their legitimacy and set out to reduce their influence over presidential nominations. To that end, the Democratic commissions, along with their Republican counterparts, eliminated *ex officio* delegates and regularized the caucus-convention system to make it less susceptible to manipulation by party professionals. At the same time, both parties deliberately fostered the participation of amateurs and political new-comers in both caucus-conventions and primaries by removing restrictive rules. These changes made it easier for unaffiliated voters to get involved in party activi-ties. In addition, the Democrats sought to increase the influence of traditionally underrepresented groups such as women, blacks, and young people in the nomina-tion process. Thus some of the most important changes in presidential politics have occurred because of conscious policies calculated to bring about the desired results.

Other changes seem not to have been deliberate. As previously shown, the McGovern-Fraser commission set out to reform the caucus-convention system in-stead of promoting the passage of new state presidential primary laws. However, the commission may have inadvertently stimulated the enactment of such primaries as a means of avoiding some of the undesirable aspects of the complicated new caucus-convention rules. There is also no indication that when the Congress enacted the new campaign finance law designed to mitigate the problems associated with tra-ditional fund raising, it deliberately calculated that providing individual candidates instead of the political parties with public funds would weaken the parties' role in the nomination and election process. And, as Jeane Kirkpatrick (1977: 29) has suggested, advocates of the primary intended to give the general public control over the nomination process and presumably did not intend to relinquish power over that process to Walter Cronkite and other "media moguls." Thus changes made in the presidential contest to accomplish certain ends frequently bring about other unin-tended consequences.

Technology has also been an important element in the changes that have taken place in the presidential contest. Of major consequence was the development of television, which has radically altered the way political appeals are communicated to the general public. Other developments, such as the use of the computer and techniques of sampling opinions of the American people, have also revolutionized the planning and conduct of political campaigns. These developments have spawned a new group of communications and public relations specialists whose talents are available to presidential candidates. As a result, candidates are able to build their own personal political organizations to undertake the vital electoral functions that they used to have to depend on traditional party organizations to perform.

Finally, a number of changes in presidential contests reflect broader social trends in American society. The increasing nationalization of American life—aided by the expansion of the mass media—tends to focus attention on national instead of state political leaders; this factor, along with the increasing importance of foreign affairs in American political life, has made senators and vice presidents more attractive presidential candidates. The relatively healthy state of the American economy and the availability of higher education to more and more citizens has helped create a broadened class of professional persons with independent political attitudes and a keen interest in political issues. This development has brought into the politics of the presidential contest a new breed of political amateurs or, as Jeane Kirkpatrick terms them, a "new presidential elite," with views that are distinct from those of party professionals and rank and file voters.*

These are the major changes that have occurred in the presidential contest and the factors that have shaped them. The next section evaluates the current method of choosing the chief executive.

EVALUATION OF THE PRESIDENTIAL CONTEST

The developments described in the previous section have created a much more democratic presidential nomination process. The growth in the number of presidential primaries, plus the passage of rules in both parties opening up caucuses and conventions to greater participation by candidate enthusiasts and rank and file voters, has ended the former domination of presidential nominations by party professionals. Moreover, both the mass media and public opinion polls have helped to sensitize candidates to public attitudes on matters pertaining to the selection process.

Presidential nominations are now also open to a wider range of candidates. Recent changes in regulations, including the public financing of a portion of the campaign costs, makes it possible for political underdogs to challenge successfully more established candidates in both parties. The results of the 1976 contest attest to the fact. An obscure, one-term governor of a southern state won the Democratic nomination; at the same time, another exgovernor battled an incumbent president down to the wire for the Republican party designation.

Although these developments in the nomination process have generally been favorable for democratic government, they nevertheless raise some major problems. The increased influence of amateurs dedicated to issue-oriented candidates means

---

*Kirkpatrick also suggests (1977: 18) that the reform rules of the Democratic party have aided this group because such rules place a premium on verbal skills, self-confidence, ideological motivations for political participation, and the possession of certain social (as contrasted to political) characteristics, such as sex, race, and age.

that both parties run the risk of nominating candidates whose views on public policy do not correlate with views of rank-and-file voters. When they do—as the Republicans did when they nominated Barry Goldwater in 1964 and the Democrats did when they chose George McGovern in 1972—the result is the mass defection of traditional party supporters and the overwhelming defeat of the party's candidate in the general election. Such landslide elections often have unfortunate results. The winning candidate, emboldened by his victory, may initiate highly questionable policies (Franklin Roosevelt tried to pack the Supreme Court following the 1936 election, and Lyndon Johnson stepped up our commitment in Vietnam after his 1964 victory). The losing party, its ranks depleted, is unable to offer effective opposition to the party in power. Another serious possibility is that the amateurs *in both parties* could be successful in the same year and confront the electorate in the November election with having to make a decision between a Goldwater and a McGovern. What would the bulk of the voters—those with middle-of-the-road views—do with such a Hobson's choice?

The augmented role of the *media* in recent presidential elections also has some unfavorable consequences. If the amateurs are primarily concerned with candidates' stands on issues, journalists seem to be preoccupied with matters of political style, in particular, how charismatic candidates are and how they appear on television. Journalists also seem disposed toward newcomers who, as "new faces," not only create more public interest than established politicians, but also tend to attack the "establishment," creating the kind of conflict that benefits the media. Candidates such as John Kennedy or Jimmy Carter are thus more newsworthy than Henry Jackson or Edmund Muskie.

Generally, the media do *not* do a good job of handling issues in presidential campaigns. This is a feature partly caused by natural limitations, especially of television. A typical story on an evening television news program consumes one and one-half minutes, hardly enough time to analyze complex social problems and the candidates' approaches to them intelligently. However, the media are also uneven in their treatment of candidates with respect to the issues. They permitted John Kennedy to implore that "we get the nation moving again" without specifying how that should be done and allowed George McGovern to suggest that all Americans, regardless of income, be given a $1000 grant without divulging just how much that would cost.* In contrast, they badgered Governor Romney to explain in great detail how he would end the war in Vietnam and asked Hubert Humphrey to spell out his precise differences with President Johnson over that same conflict.

Both political amateurs and the major journalists also tend *not to be representative* of the average American. As Jeane Kirkpatrick has pointed out, the "new presidential elite" is a highly professional class with views on public policy, par-

---

*Although the media eventually criticized this proposal, they virtually ignored it during the early months of the nomination campaign when McGovern was winning some of his crucial primary victories.

ticularly on social and cultural issues, that vary greatly from the views of the average voter. Journalist David Broder (1973: 29) also acknowledges that the small number (he gave a figure at the time of a "couple of dozen") of political reporters working for major news organizations committed to the coverage of national politics are Easterners by residence, between the ages of thirty and forty-five, well-paid, white, tend to vote Democratic, and do not attend church regularly. Even though he deliberately chooses not to comment on their social, political, or ethical views, Broder indicates that such reporters "represent a narrow and rather peculiar slice of society."

What is perhaps most disturbing is that neither political amateurs nor media representatives are *responsive* and *accountable* to the American public. Amateurs generally come into politics for the purpose of seeing that candidates who espouse their own policy views are chosen for the presidency; once that is either accomplished or fails to occur, they return to their private lives. Media representatives are in a similar situation. Once the presidential contest is over, they go about their regular business. In many cases, they criticize the candidates they formerly favored, because the successful contenders are now part of the "establishment," which is a favorite target of journalists.

Party professionals are generally more responsive and accountable as far as presidential nominations are concerned. Since they are in public life on a more permanent basis and want to remain in office if they can, professionals are likely to be sensitive and concerned about public sentiments. They also have a stake in ensuring that the person nominated and elected as president will reflect well on their party. Moreover, if their presidential candidate is elected, they continue to take an interest in what that person is doing. Those who hold public office themselves work with the president on the nation's problems, and so they are a potential source of political support, as well as restraint, on the chief executive.

I am not suggesting by this discussion that political amateurs and media representatives be eliminated from the presidential nomination process. The amateur's concern with issues is a healthy development in the democratic system. The media's focus on the personality and communication skills of presidential candidates is important, because such attributes are considerations in choosing a chief executive. But I do feel that party professionals should also play an important role in the process, because they bring distinctive peer perspectives to bear on presidential candidacies: an assessment on how effectively individuals can work with other public officials with whom they must share the governance of the nation and how successful they are likely to be in helping to compromise the differences that exist among the many increasingly assertive groups in our society. For these reasons, I favor correcting the imbalance in the nomination process that presently exists in favor of amateurs and media representatives and against party professionals. This matter will be discussed in the concluding section of this chapter.

I am not as concerned about the role that political amateurs and the mass media play in presidential elections as I am about their part in the nomination process. Although their respective motives and biases remain the same, their effect is less pronounced. It is easier for amateurs to dominate sparsely attended caucuses and conventions or even some presidential primaries with light turnouts than it is to prevail in general elections with an expanded electorate. (Note how poorly Barry Goldwater and George McGovern did in the 1964 and 1972 contests.) Furthermore, the media is in a much better position to influence public attitudes in the early, unstructured stages of the nomination process, when many candidates are involved, than during the fall campaign, when voters have fuller information on the personal backgrounds and issue orientations of the two major party candidates, as well as party labels that serve as cues as to how they should cast their ballot. (Richard Nixon's presidential campaign of 1968 is reputed to be the perfect example of the use of television for image building, but his support among the electorate did not rise during the campaign; however, Humphrey who, because of financial limitations, made far less use of television than Nixon, gained ground rapidly, especially in the last stages of the campaign.)

There were some distinct improvements in the 1976 presidential campaigns. The new campaign finance law providing public subsidies to the major party candidate equalized the resources available to the candidates and spared them the problems and dangers associated with raising funds from private groups and individuals. The presidential debates helped to acquaint the electorate with the candidates' views on a variety of political issues. The debates also enabled observers to judge the personal qualities of Ford and Carter. The first debate to be held between vice-presidential candidates also provided voters with some clues as to how Robert Dole and Walter Mondale might perform if tragic circumstances forced one of them into the presidency.

Despite the fears expressed by many persons that media campaigns help devious candidates to manipulate the American public into making voting decisions based on irrelevant considerations, the electoral process has actually become more rational in recent years. The presidential candidates and the major parties give clearer signals to the electorate than they formerly did on their stands on the major issues. As a result, voters are better able to distinguish between the general public policy approaches used by the contending groups. The voters themselves have also become more consistent in their attitudes toward a range of issues. People now pay close attention to the personal backgrounds of the candidates and are willing to vote a party representative out of office if they are dissatisfied with how the nation's affairs have been handled. Thus V. O. Key's (1967: 7-8) major conclusion of more than a decade ago that "voters are not fools" and that the electorate is "moved by concerns about central and relevant questions of public policy, government performance, and of executive personality" has been confirmed and, if anything, is more true today than it was at the time he made it.

Thus American presidential campaigns and elections do meet many of the democratic functions suggested in the Introduction. The "great search committee" for the nation's major political leader has become greatly expanded over the years. Our electoral process has also given voters the ability to correct their past mistakes by "throwing the rascals out," as evidenced by the fact that Republican and Democratic presidents have evenly divided the eight administrations since World War II. Moreover, as previously mentioned, the presidential candidates have identified many of our major social problems and proposed policies and programs for dealing with them. The record on the last two theoretical functions of democratic campaigns and elections—that they serve as a catharsis by bringing societal conflicts out in the open and that this process may help develop attitudes of political compromise and further social consensus—is less clear. However, it is at least arguable that between the presidential elections of 1968 and 1972, the nation faced up to the trauma of the Vietnam tragedy and eventually developed a compromise course of action for dealing with it (systematic withdrawal over time instead of either a greater American commitment or immediate departure) that most of the public was willing to support.

There are, however, some disquieting features of recent presidential contests. One is the decline since 1960 in voter participation in general elections. Although it is, of course, possible to attribute this decline to a general public satisfaction with the situation in the United States (if things are going well, why bother to vote?), most of the evidence is to the contrary. People have become discouraged over the unresponsiveness of the American political system to their needs and are also dissatisfied with the caliber of our political leaders.

At this point it is difficult to make a sound judgment on how permanent these phenomena may be. Rising public expectations in the 1960s and 1970s about the government's ability to handle the myriad problems of our highly complex society, along with the twin shocks of Vietnam and Watergate, greatly disillusioned voters in these two decades. It is possible that as the memories of these two tragedies fade and our political leaders and the American public become more realistic about our ability to find instant solutions to difficult problems, some of the traditional public confidence will be restored in our public institutions. If that happens, we may reasonably expect voting participation to rise in presidential elections.

It is also possible that at least part of the recent decline in participation in presidential general elections is due to changes in the presidential contest itself. As indicated in Chapter 2, the trend is toward more, not less, voters exercising their right to vote in state presidential primaries, particularly when major rival candidates are in contention. Thus, in recent years, more persons have participated in presidential primaries, but fewer have participated in presidential general elections. It is conceivable that an increasing number of voters attempt to influence the choice of the president through the nomination process and, when their favored candidate loses, do not bother to vote in the general election. It is also possible that the protracted nature of the selection process that today extends over a longer period than it formerly did is wearisome to part of the American public, so that by the time the general election takes place, they are not inclined to take the time and effort to vote.

One final feature of presidential elections that I feel constitutes a major problem is the operation of the electoral college system. As indicated in Chapter 3, it advantages voters who live in very large and very small states, particularly where there is close competition between the two major political parties. Even more serious is the fact that the college can operate to deny the electoral victory to the candidate who wins the nationwide popular vote. For example, even though Jimmy Carter received a 1.7 million popular plurality over Gerald Ford in 1976, if about 9000 voters in Hawaii and Ohio had shifted their ballots to President Ford, he would have edged out Carter in the electoral college 270 to 268. Moreover, in three other recent elections, similar shifts would have denied the immediate electoral victory to the popular-vote winner and thrown the election into the House of Representatives, where the president would have been chosen under a system in which each state delegation, regardless of size, would have had one vote. This result would have occurred in 1948 if about 12,000 people in California and Ohio had voted for Thomas Dewey instead of Harry Truman; in 1960, if approximately 9000 persons in Illinois and Missouri had cast their ballots for Richard Nixon instead of John Kennedy; and again in 1968 if around 42,000 persons in Alaska, New Jersey, and Missouri had voted for Hubert Humphrey instead of Nixon.* Other problems arising from the present electoral college system and proposals for changing that system are discussed in the final section of this chapter.

IMPROVING THE PRESIDENTIAL CONTEST

The current system of choosing presidential nominees is highly pluralistic. It draws on the diverse experiences and perspectives of party professionals, political amateurs, and journalists who help to screen the various candidates. At the same time, it ensures that the preference of rank-and-file voters will determine the final choice of the nominee. It therefore represents a variety of interests that have a legitimate concern in the selection of the nation's highest public official.

However, as indicated in the previous section, I feel that the system has become somewhat imbalanced in recent years. Specifically, it gives too little credence to the views of the professionals who are uniquely suited to make peer judgments on how effective nominees will be in working with other public officials and in helping to mitigate and compromise the many demands made by increasingly assertive groups in our complex society. At the same time, I see no easy way to change the situation. It is unrealistic to expect states that have adopted presidential

*In all these elections, persons other than the two major candidates received electoral votes; therefore, Dewey, Nixon, and Humphrey could have carried the cited states and still not have had a majority of the electoral votes.

primaries to abandon them now; even if they did, and they returned to the caucus-convention system that they formerly used, there is no assurance that political amateurs would not dominate such meetings as they have lately done in so many states. Perhaps the best approach to the problem is to provide specifically for greater representation of the professionals in the nomination process. The Democratic National Committee has recently done this by adopting a rule for 1980 to increase the size of state delegations by 10 percent in order to accommodate state party and elected officials.* My own preference would be to see that figure raised to 20 or 25 percent and the same principle adopted by the Republican party. It is also possible that limiting participation in delegate-selection to party members only (as the Democrats have also done for 1980) will increase the influence of professionals in the nomination process.

The presidential nomination process would be greatly improved if the media would change some of its practices. As F. Christopher Arterton (1978: 51–54) suggests, the news organizations could assign reporters to state contests, not to a single candidate ("zone" instead of "candidate coverage"); such a change would avoid the possibility of media representatives' becoming coopted by and uncritical of a candidate and would also broaden their perspective of the nomination campaign. It would also be helpful if there were less "pack journalism"; local reporters and editors should have more confidence in their own interpretations of nomination contests in their states instead of parroting the views of national reporters and columnists. The American public would benefit from receiving the divergent views of a range of journalists on the different presidential candidates.

The media should also stop concentrating on the "horse race" aspect of presidential nominations and devote more effort to giving in-depth information on the issues of the campaign. Although the time limitations and the lack of serious political interest of most television viewers preclude that medium's performing that function very well, there is no reason why radio and the print media cannot do so. The media should also do a better job of assigning substantive specialists (persons trained in law and economics, for example) to analyze the candidates' public policy proposals. They should also try to be more evenhanded in their evaluation of the proposals put forth by various candidates, not expecting some to explain their ideas in detail, but allowing others to be less specific.

I also believe that the media can do a better job of investigating the personal backgrounds of the candidates. I do not share James David Barber's (1978b: 148) optimism about the ability of journalists to make psychological judgments about presidential candidates that will provide very reliable predictions about how they will perform in office, but I do agree with him that journalists should look "past the upcoming primary to the presidency itself," and try to decide which qualities are

---

*Beginning in 1974, the Democratic party provided for such officials attending national conventions, but not as voting delegates, as those included in the 10 percent will be.

most important for a chief executive to possess (Barber, 1978a: 145). I also believe that political reporters should investigate more thoroughly how well presidential candidates did in previous public offices and also try to find out more about their close associates, campaign managers, and aides (such as Haldeman and Jordan), since these people often end up in key administrative positions if their candidate wins the presidency. The vice-presidential candidates should also receive closer scrutiny from the media, since one of them may succeed to the presidential office.

Finally, I would hope that the media would stop focusing so much attention on the very early state contests; Donald Matthews (1978: 65) reports that in 1976 "the three national networks presented 100 stories on the New Hampshire primary or exactly 2.63 stores per delegate selected there!" I also believe that they would perform a public service if they stopped employing the winner-take-all principle by which the winning candidate in a state primary or caucus-convention is given virtually all the publicity, regardless of how narrow the victory is or how few popular votes or convention delegates are involved. The same is true of the media's tendency to declare candidates who win early contests as having clearly established themselves as the leading contenders for the presidential nomination. Such practices seriously mislead the American public and create a self-fulfilling prophecy that is unfair to aspirants who do not do well in the very early stages of the nomination.

Of course, it is easy for a political scientist to tell journalists how to run their affairs. It may be that at least some of these suggestions, particularly the ones that deal with the media's handling of early state contests, are not feasible because they are inconsistent with the needs of a highly competitive industry that thrives on excitement and drama. Another possibility would be to restructure the nomination process so that one state could not hold its primary earlier than other states, as New Hampshire has traditionally done. This could be accomplished by requiring all states that use presidential primaries to schedule them on four or five specific dates. Another possibility would be to cluster those primaries by geographical regions of the country, as Senator Packwood has recently proposed, with the order in which these regional primaries are held to be determined by lot.

The regional primary approach would also have other advantages besides blunting the influence of the media. As Donald Johnson (1976: 20) suggests, it would reduce the travel time and physical punishment to the candidates who could personally campaign in a single region instead of being forced, as Edmund Muskie was in 1972, to visit Illinois, Florida, and New Hampshire in one weekend. The political appeal of the candidates would also be assessed on the basis of how they did in a number of states that hold simultaneous primaries and not on their performance in a single, small state like New Hampshire.

I would favor changing the present system to provide for a series of regional contests for the states that wanted to hold primaries, but I would be very much opposed to the adoption of a direct national primary to nominate our presidential candidates. Even though this system would have certain advantages—mainly its directness and simplicity compared to the present hodgepodge of primaries and caucus-convention contests with widely differing legal provisions relating to the selection of delegates—such benefits would be outweighed by a number of unfavorable consequences that would probably occur if a direct national primary were adopted. It would eliminate the possibility of a lesser-known candidate's making a relatively limited investment of money and effort in key state primaries and, having won them, going on to take the nomination from well-established political figures who rated high in the public opinion polls at the beginning of the election year. The system would thus be less open than the present one. A national primary in which a large number of persons were entered (this has been the recent pattern, particularly in the party out of power) could also result in the winning candidate's receiving only 20 to 25 percent of the vote. That possibility could be avoided by requiring a runoff between the top two contenders, but then candidates would have to make three nationwide campaigns (including the general election) within a fairly short period. A nationwide contest would probably also increase the role of the media in the nomination process (candidates would be forced more than they are now to use the mass media in order to reach a national audience), with the previously discussed problems associated with media influence. Finally, I agree with Austin Ranney (1978b: 35–36) that extending the primary to all states would probably deliver "the final blow" to our already "very sick" parties, a consequence much to be regretted.

There is, however, one basic feature of our present nomination system that definitely must be changed: the selection of vice president. Recent experiences with the Republican choice of Spiro Agnew (who resigned from office in disgrace) and Thomas Eagleton (who was forced off the Democratic ticket because of previous mental illness) indicate the flaws in the present custom of leaving the matter completely to the discretion of the presidential nominee (who often makes a quick decision on his running mate less than twenty-four hours after he has been chosen).* Among the possibilities for improvement are having leading contenders appoint informal committees to help them screen potential vice-presidential candidates before the convention and, if necessary, extending the period in which the presidential nominee has to make the decision so that he has enough time to obtain the information required for an informed choice. Another idea worth considering would be to involve other groups in the process formally. For example, the presidential nominee might submit a list of three or four persons who are acceptable and let the convention delegates or the national committee make the final selection.

I also believe that some improvements should be made in the general election campaign. Two of them build on desirable features of the 1976 contest. The first concerns the financing of the campaign. As indicated, I favor the system of public subsidies because it equalizes the financial resources available to the major party

---

*Carter's careful personal screening of vice-presidential candidates in 1976 was possible because he had the nomination wrapped up several weeks before the convention.

candidates and frees them from the necessity of raising funds from wealthy party contributors. However, the full public subsidy deprived citizens in 1976 of the opportunity to donate funds and services to their favorite presidential candidate and also cut down that year on traditional party activities at the grass roots level. I would favor using the same approach in general elections that is now employed in the nomination phase of the presidential contest: allow candidates to raise some of their support from private individuals and groups (other than just political action committees), but place an overall limit on campaign expenditures and make the partial federal financing contingent on the raising of moneys from small contributors. The limitation on total campaign expenditures ($25 million in 1976) should also be raised to reflect the rising costs of using the mass media to communicate with voters.

The second improvement relates to the presidential debates. As I stated before, I believe the debates educated the American public on the issues and qualifications of Ford and Carter. Without the debates, voters would have known far less about the two candidates, especially since the $25 million campaign limitation restricted the amount of information that the electorate received through traditional means. Such debates should be retained, but the role of journalists in them should be reduced. Other knowledgeable persons, such as economists, political scientists, or public officials, should be included among the questioners, and the candidates themselves should be permitted to ask questions of each other.

My major suggestion for improving the presidential election has to do with the electoral college. As noted, it favors voters in very small and very large states, particularly politically competitive ones, and disadvantages those in other areas of the nation. Also, the college creates the possibility that the candidate receiving the most popular votes will not become president, either because the runner-up receives a majority of the electoral vote and assumes the office immediately, or because no candidate wins a majority of the electoral votes, and the House of Representatives, choosing from the three receiving the highest number of electoral votes, does not select the popular-vote winner.

Longley and Braun (1975: Chap. 1) emphasize three other basic problems with the electoral college. One is that of *faithless elector*, the fact that persons who actually cast the votes for president do not have to vote for the candidate who receives the most popular votes in their state. Although they generally do, there have been several defecting electors in recent elections. The situation was particularly dangerous in 1968, when the prospects of a close election raised the distinct possibility that neither Richard Nixon nor Hubert Humphrey would earn a majority of the electoral votes and the election would be thrown into the House of Representatives for a decision. (As mentioned before, if 42,000 people had switched their votes from Nixon to Humphrey, that result would actually have taken place.) George Wallace, the American party candidate, would then have been in a position to prevent a House decision from occurring by asking his electors (he eventually won 45 electoral votes in five states)* to vote for one of the two major party candidates. Thus the legal independence of presidential electors raises the possibility of their being used for political bargaining purposes.

Another problem with the electoral college arises from the general ticket or *winner-take-all* feature whereby all the electoral votes of a state go to the candidate who wins a plurality of the popular votes, no matter how narrow that margin of victory. It is possible for candidates to receive one more vote than their major rivals in a state such as California and win all 45 of its electoral votes (one-sixth of the 270 votes required for election). For people who cast their vote for the loser, it is as if they had not voted at all. In noncompetitive states there is no incentive for either major party's supporters to turn out at the polls: for those in the minority situation, their vote is futile; for those on the majority side, it is unnecessary.

Finally, there are problems that develop from the electoral college's provision for a *contingent election* if no candidate receives a majority of the electoral votes. There is the initial question of why persons elected to serve in the House of Representatives should be choosing their constitutional rival, the president. Also, the "one state delegation-one vote" procedure means that 76 members of Congress from the twenty-six smallest states with a combined 1970 population of 34.5 million could outvote 359 members representing twenty-four states with 168.7 million residents. Moreover, if such a procedure should actually occur, it could place some Representatives in a difficult position: for whom should they vote if the presidential candidate from the opposite political party carried their state or even more particularly, their congressional district?

These problems have created a great deal of dissatisfaction with the electoral college over the years. The sentiment for changing it has increased recently, especially after the elections of 1948, 1960, 1968, and 1976, in which a switch in votes of a comparatively few people in key states would have sent the selection of the president into the House or immediately changed the result. Although there is widespread agreement on the necessity for changing the electoral college, there is marked disagreement over the form of that change. Four basic plans have been suggested as substitutes for the present system.

The first, known as the *automatic plan,* would make the least change in the present system. It would eliminate the possibility of faithless electors by abolishing the office and automatically casting a state's electoral votes for the popular-vote winner. If no candidate received a majority of the electoral votes, a joint session of Congress would choose the winner, with each representative and senator having one vote.

The second, known as the *district plan,* proposes a return to the method the states used early in our history (and that was recently reinstated by Maine). This

---

*He actually received forty-six because one elector in North Carolina (which went for Nixon) cast that vote for the Alabama governor.

would mean that the presidential candidate who received the plurality vote in each House district would receive its electoral vote, and the remaining two electoral votes would go to the statewide popular winner. If no candidate received a majority of the electoral votes, senators and representatives, sitting jointly and voting as individuals, would choose the president from the three candidates having the highest number of electoral votes. This plan's major supporters have been members of Congress and private groups from rural areas such as the American Farm Bureau. If the plan were adopted, the crucial areas would be the approximately seventy-five politically competitive congressional districts where the two major parties traditionally divide the vote 55 to 45 percent.

A third proposal, known as the *proportional plan,* would divide each state's electoral votes in proportion to the division of the popular votes. If candidates received 60 percent of the popular votes in the state, they would receive 60 percent of its electoral votes. A plan of this type introduced by Republican Senator Henry Cabot Lodge of Massachusetts and Democratic Congressman Ed Gosset of Texas passed the Senate in 1950, but failed to be enacted by the House. The plan would eliminate the present advantage of the large states of being able to give all their electoral votes to one candidate. It has therefore been opposed by many of their legislators, including John Kennedy when he was a senator from Massachusetts. One possible consequence of a proportional division of the electoral votes would be a fairly even split between the two major candidates so that neither received a majority; hence there would be a greater likelihood of elections being given to Congress for a decision.*

The fourth plan, *direct popular election* of the president, has recently picked up a lot of support, especially since it was recommended in 1967 by a special commission of the American Bar Association. In addition, it has been endorsed by politically disparate groups such as the Chamber of Commerce of the United States and the AFL-CIO. In 1969 the House passed a constitutional amendment providing that the president and vice president be elected by a minimum of 40 percent of the popular vote. If no candidate received so large a vote, a runoff would be held between the two front-runners. The Senate failed to pass the amendment, however, despite the efforts of its major sponsor, Birch Bayh, a Democrat from Indiana. After Carter's narrow electoral college victory in 1976, Bayh introduced the same measure in 1977, but even though it has the support of the president himself this time, the measure has yet to clear either the Senate or the House.

In my judgment the first three plans have serious defects that should (and probably will) prevent their adoption. The automatic plan meets only the faithless

---

*Most of the proportional plans have suggested lowering the winning electoral-vote requirement from a majority to 40 or even 35 percent to avoid the possibility of having the election go to the House. They have also proposed that, if no candidate receives the requisite proportion of electoral votes, the two houses, meeting jointly and voting as individuals, choose the president.

elector and, to some extent, the contingent election problems and ignores the others—undue influence of the very small and very large states, winner-take-all principle, and possibility of the minority-vote president. The district plan would incorporate into the selection of the president the gerrymandering abuses that still remain despite the reapportionment decisions—manipulating House district boundaries (including noncompact, noncontiguous ones) to favor particular political interests. The proportional plan would eliminate the winner-take-all advantage presently enjoyed by the large states but would retain the small-state benefit, because all states, regardless of size, receive two electoral votes representing their two senators; it also would not prevent the possibility of a minority-vote president. As Longley and Braun (p. 66) point out, the only proposed plan that solves all the problems of the electoral college is the one providing for the direct popular election of the president. There is general agreement today between both the opponents and defenders of the electoral college system that, if it is to be replaced, it will be by the direct election method.

Defenders of the present system register a number of objections to the direct election of the president. One basic fault they find with the new plan is its failure to protect minority interests as the electoral college does. Sometimes their concern is with minority interests in general, which are thought to be protected by the principles of federalism built into the present electoral system (Best, 1975: Chap. 7). In other instances, particular minority groups are singled out for special solicitude, such as those who live in metropolitan areas (Sayre and Parris, 1970: Chap. 8). One basis of the special concern for residents of these areas is that the nation's greatest social problems tend to be concentrated there; another is that rural areas are often overrepresented in Congress. As compensation, the urban—or more specifically, the metropolitan areas—should be overrepresented in the selection of the president.

I find neither of these arguments very persuasive. Federalism is indeed an important feature of our constitutional system. Its principles are already implemented in the equal representation of the states in the Senate and in the arrangement of separate state powers and political institutions whose independence is protected from national encroachment by a written constitution. I see no reason why federalism should also require that states be represented as units in the selection of our only major national official. As far as metropolitan areas are concerned, it is precisely the suburban areas of most rapid growth that are gaining greater representation in the House of Representatives since the reapportionment decisions of the 1960s. This being the case, I do not see why they should also remain the most overrepresented areas in presidential selection, as they are in the electoral college system (Longley, 1977: 18).* Moreover, no group or state should receive special

---

*Many persons assume that blacks are advantaged by the electoral college, but Longley's (1977: 16) analysis shows that they are actually hurt by it, primarily because so many blacks continue to live in the South, a region of mainly medium-sized states disadvantaged by the present system.

consideration in the selection of presidents; they should represent all the American people equally, no matter where they live.

Another basic concern of defenders of the electoral college is that the direct popular election of the president will jeopardize our two-party system. This fear is based on two separate considerations. One is that since the election will depend on a nationwide instead of a state-by-state vote, candidates will no longer need to deal with state political leaders; this factor would weaken these leaders, who have traditionally played such a vital role in American political parties. The second concern, expressed by Alexander Bickel (1968: 14–16), is that direct popular election of the president will encourage minor political parties, freed of the necessity of actually winning state electoral votes, to run and support enough candidates to prevent either major party nominee from winning the necessary 40 percent of the nationwide popular vote. These minor parties would then be in a bargaining position to determine which of the two leading candidates will win in the runoff election. Thus presidential contests would become like the unstructured, faction-laden Democratic primaries described by V.O. Key (1949) in his study of Southern politics.

Again, I believe these fears are unfounded. State party leaders will continue to play a role in presidential nominations. It is even possible that they would become more active in the general election under a popular election system, since all votes that they could muster would count in their candidate's nationwide total. I also think it highly improbable that the winning party candidate would not be able to win 40 percent of the popular vote. As Longley and Braun (1975: Chap. 2) point out, in the thirty-nine presidential elections held since 1824, only Abraham Lincoln in 1860 failed to achieve that proportion (he won 39.8 percent of the vote).* If anything, the electoral college system is more vulnerable than a popular election system to minor parties, because in the United States such parties tend to be regional and thus best able to affect the distribution of electoral votes of individual states. A recent case in point occurred in New York in 1976. If Eugene McCarthy been able to get on the ballot there, many observers feel he would have drained away enough popular votes from Carter to allow Ford to carry the state and, with it, enough electoral votes (forty-one) to have won the presidential election. Moreover, I feel that Bickel's analogy between interparty competition in presidential elections and that involving gubernatorial primaries is false. The presidential candidates benefit from traditional loyalties passed on through the socialization process, but state factional leaders do not.

A final major problem† cited by supporters of the electoral college is the effect

---

*Neil Peirce (1968: 295) also cites figures compiled by Donald Stokes showing that in 170 gubernatorial elections occurring in the thirty most competitive states between 1952 and 1964 (these contests, of course, involved direct popular election), the winning candidate never received less than 40 percent of the popular vote.

†Two other arguments that the electoral college is desirable because it presently amplifies close

that the adoption of the direct popular election of the president would have on the nomination process. As Austin Ranney (1978a: 4) suggests, most of the arguments made against the electoral college and in favor of direct national elections can also be made against national party conventions and in favor of a direct national primary. Both the electoral college and national conventions violate the one-person, one-vote rule, make it possible to choose a candidate preferred by a minority, and place artificial barriers between the people and their choice of candidates. Although Ranney does not make the point explicitly, it might well be argued that the adoption of the direct election of the president would logically lead in time to a similar enactment of a national primary law: historically, the number of electoral votes a state has affected the size of its delegation to national conventions. Thus the selection and nomination processes have been linked and tampering with one might influence the other.

I confess that the last possibility gives me the greatest cause for concern, particularly since, as previously discussed, I do not favor the adoption of a national primary. I do feel, however, that the two processes are distinct, and changing one does not necessarily mean altering the other. Moving from the electoral college system to a direct popular election of the president would not be nearly so radical a change as abandoning the convention system for a national presidential primary. The first alternative does not significantly change the method of selection or the people participating in the election of the president: it merely changes how the votes are *counted*. However, a change in the presidential nominating system would substitute a whole new method of selection and bring new persons into the process who are not now eligible to vote in presidential primaries. It would also involve developing some new means of choosing vice-presidential candidates and of adopting the party platform. Hopefully, it would be much more difficult to convince political decision makers to adopt a national primary than to move to a direct popular election of the president. No broad range of groups similar to those favoring the direct election of the president has surfaced to support a national primary; the first was recently passed by the House, and the second has not been given serious consideration by Congress.

In the final analysis, the known defects of the present electoral college system must be weighed against the possible dangers that the direct election of the president might bring, particularly its potential effect on the nomination process. I for one would be willing to take the gamble associated with change. I cannot see the

----

popular election outcomes (Diamond, 1977: 16) and that direct popular election would increase the possibility of vote fraud (Best, 1975: Chap. 6), I do not feel are significant. Justifying a distortion of the actual election results to create a false mandate seems curious. Moreover, the effects of vote fraud are more likely to be felt at the state than the national level; in 1976, 9000 false ballots in Hawaii and Ohio could have reversed Carter's electoral victory, but it would have taken almost 100 times that number to have eliminated his 1.7 million nationwide popular plurality.

wisdom of perpetuating an electoral system that in 1976 almost permitted an appointed chief executive, who lost his only presidential election by almost 2 million votes, to remain in office for another term. Our political system, already subject to a great deal of cynicism by the American people, should not have to bear that additional threat to its legitimacy.

REFERENCES

Adamany, David (1972). *Campaign Finance in America*. North Scituate, Mass.: Duxbury.

——— (1976). "Cross-over Voting and the Democratic Party's Reform Rules." *American Political Science Review, 70* (June): 536–541.

Agranoff, Robert (1976). *The Management of Election Campaigns*. Boston: Holbrook Press.

Alexander, Herbert (1976). *Financing Politics, Money, Elections and Political Reform*. Washington, D.C.: Congressional Quarterly Press.

Asher, Herbert (1976). *Presidential Elections and American Politics: Voters, Candidates, and Campaigns Since 1952*. Homewood, Ill.: Dorsey.

Arterton, F. Christopher (1978). "The Media Politics of Presidential Campaigns: A Study of the Carter Nomination Drive," in James David Barber (ed.), *Race for the Presidency: The Media and the Nominating Process*. Englewood Cliffs, N.J.: Prentice-Hall.

Barber, James David (1978a). "Characters in the Campaign: The Literary Problem," in James David Barber (ed.), *Race for the Presidency: The Media and the Nominating Process*. Englewood Cliffs, N.J.: Prentice-Hall.

——— (1978b). "Characters in the Campaign: The Scientific Question," in James David Barber (ed.), *Race for the Presidency: The Media and the Nominating Process*. Englewood Cliffs, N.J.: Prentice-Hall.

Best, Judith (1975). *The Case Against the Direct Election of the President: A Defense of the Electoral College*. Ithaca, N.Y.: Cornell University Press.

Bickel, Alexander (1968). *The New Age of Political Reform: The Electoral College, the Convention, and the Party System*. New York: Harper & Row.

Bicker, William (1978). "Network Television News and the 1976 Presidential Primaries: A Look from the Networks' Side of the Camera," in James David Barber (ed.), *Race for the Presidency: The Media and the Nominating Process*. Englewood Cliffs, N.J.: Prentice-Hall.

Broder, David (1973). "Political Reporters in Presidential Politics," in Charles Peters and John Rothchild (eds.), *Inside the System: A Washington Monthly Book*. New York: Praeger.

Campbell, Angus, Philip Converse, Warren Miller, and Donald Stokes (1964). *The American Voter* (an abridgement). New York: Wiley.

——— (1966). *Elections and the Political Order*. New York: Wiley.

Campbell, Angus, Gerald Gurin, and Warren Miller (1954). *The Voter Decides*. Evanston, Ill.: Row, Peterson.

Cantril, Albert, and Charles Roll (1971). *Hopes and Fears of the American People*. New York: Universe Books.

Ceasar, James (1978). "Political Parties and Presidential Ambition." *Journal of Politics, 40* (August): 708–739.

Chambers, William (1963). *Political Parties in a New Nation: The American Experience, 1776–1809*. New York: Oxford.

Charles, Joseph (1956). *The Origins of the American Party System*. New York: Harper Torchbooks (Harper & Row).

Chester, Lewis, Godfrey Hodgson, and Bruce Page (1969). *An American Melodrama: The Presidential Campaign of 1968*. New York: Viking.

Congressional Quarterly (1975). *Presidential Elections Since 1789*. Washington, D.C.: Congressional Quarterly Press.

Converse, Philip (1976). *The Dynamics of Party Support: Cohort-Analyzing Party Identification*. Beverly Hills, Calif.: Sage.

——— (1964). "The Nature of Belief Systems in Mass Publics," in David Apter (ed.), *Ideology and Discontent*. New York: Free Press.

Crotty, William (1977). *Political Reform and the American Experiment*. New York: Crowell.

Crouse, Timothy (1972). *The Boys on the Bus*. New York: Ballantine Books (Random House).

David, Paul, Ralph Goldman, and Richard Bain, paperback rev. ed. by Kathleen Sproul (1964). *The Politics of National Party Conventions*. Washington, D.C.: Brookings.

Davis, James (1967). *Presidential Primaries: Road to the White House*. New York: Crowell.

DeVries, Walter, and Lance Tarrance (1972). *The Ticket Splitter: A New Force in American Politics*. Grand Rapids, Mich.: William B. Eerdmans.

Diamond, Martin (1977). *The Electoral College and the American Idea of Democracy*. Washington, D.C.: American Enterprise Institute.

Epstein, Leon (1978). "Political Science and Presidential Nominations." *Political Science Quarterly, 93* (Summer): 177–195.

Farrand, Max (1913). *The Framing of the Constitution of the United States*. New Haven, Conn.: Yale University Press.

Hadley, Arthur (1976). *The Invisible Primary*. Englewood Cliffs, N.J.: Prentice-Hall.

Heard, Alexander (1960). *The Costs of Democracy*. Garden City, N.Y.: Anchor (Doubleday).

Heclo, Hugh (1973). "Presidential and Prime Ministerial Selection," in Donald R. Matthews (ed.), *Perspectives on Presidential Selection*. Washington, D.C.: Brookings.

Hedlund, Ronald, and Meredith Watts (1977). "Voting in an Open Primary." Paper delivered at the annual meeting of American Political Science Association.

Hess, Stephen (1974). *The Presidential Campaign*. Washington, D.C.: Brookings.

Janowitz, Morris, and Dwaine Marvick (1956). *Competitive Pressure and Democratic Consent*. Ann Arbor: Bureau of Government, Institute of Public Administration, University of Michigan.

Jewell, Malcolm, and David Olson (1978). *American State Political Parties and Elections*. Homewood, Ill.: Dorsey.

Johnson, Donald (1976). *The Politics of Delegate Selection*. New York: The Robert A. Taft Institute of Government.

Keech, William, and Donald Matthews (1976). *The Party's Choice*. Washington, D.C.: Brookings.

Kessel, John (1968). *The Goldwater Coalition: Republican Strategies in 1964*. Indianapolis: Bobbs-Merrill.

——— (1974). "Strategy for November," in James Barber (ed.), *Choosing the President*. Englewood Cliffs, N.J.: Prentice-Hall.

Key, V.O., Jr. (1949). *Southern Politics in State and Nation*. New York: Knopf.

——— (1956). *American State Politics: An Introduction*. New York: Knopf.

Key, V.O., Jr., with the assistance of Milton Cummings (1966). *The Responsible Electorate: Rationality in Presidential Voting, 1936–1960*. Cambridge, Mass.: Belknap Press (Harvard University Press).

Kirkpatrick, Jeane (1976). *The New Presidential Elite: Men and Women in National Politics*. New York: Russel Sage Foundation and The Twentieth Century Fund.

———— (1977). "Dismantling the Parties: Reflections on the Role of Policy in the Process of Party Decomposition." Paper Delivered at the Annual Meeting of American Political Science Association.

Ladd, Everett (1978). *Where Have All the Voters Gone?* New York: Norton.

Lazarsfeld, Paul, Bernard Berelson, and Hazel Gaudet (1944). *The People's Choice.* New York: Columbia University Press.

Lazarsfeld, Paul, Bernard Berelson, and William McPhee (1954). *Voting.* Chicago: University of Chicago Press.

Lengle, James, and Byron Shafer (1976). "Primary Rules, Political Power and Social Change." *American Political Science Review, LXX* (March): 25–40.

Leuthold, David (1968). *Electioneering in a Democracy: Campaigns for Congress.* New York: Wiley.

Longley, Lawrence, and Alan Braun (1975). *The Politics of Electoral College Reform.* New Haven, Conn.: Yale University Press.

Longley, Lawrence (1977). "The Case Against the Electoral College." Paper delivered at the annual meeting of American Political Science Association.

Matthews, Donald (1974). "Presidential Nominations: Process and Outcomes," in James Barber (ed.), *Choosing the President.* Englewood Cliffs, N.J.: Prentice-Hall.

———— (1978). "Winnowing: The News Media and the 1976 Presidential Nominations," in James David Barber (ed.), *Race for the Presidency: The Media and the Nominating Process.* Englewood Cliffs, N.J.: Prentice-Hall.

May, Ernest, and Janet Fraser (1973). *Campaign '72: The Managers Speak.* Cambridge, Mass.: Harvard University Press.

McCluhan, Marshall (1964). *Understanding Media.* New York: McGraw-Hill.

Miller, Arthur, and Warren Miller (1977). "Partisanship and Performance: Rational Choice in the 1976 Presidential Election." Paper delivered at the annual meeting of American Political Science Association.

Miller, Warren, and Teresa Levitin (1976). *Leadership and Change: The New Politics and the American Electorate.* Cambridge, Mass.: Winthrop.

Moore, Jonathan, and Janet Fraser (eds.) 1977. *Campaign for President: The Managers Look at '76.* Cambridge, Mass.: Ballinger.

Morris, William, and O. Davis (1975). "The Sport of Kings: Turnout in Presidential Preference Primaries." Paper prepared for annual meeting of American Political Science Association.

Nie, Norman, and Kristi Andersen (1974). "Mass Belief Systems Revisited: Political Change and Attitude Structure." *Journal of Politics, 36* (August): 540–591.

Nie, Norman, Sidney Verba, and John Petrocik (1976). *The Changing American Voter.* Cambridge, Mass.: Harvard University Press.

Nimmo, Dan (1970). *The Political Persuaders: The Techniques of Modern Election Campaigns.* Englewood Cliffs, N.J.: Prentice Hall.

Parris, Judith (1972). *The Convention Problem: Issues in Reform of Presidential Nominating Procedures.* Washington, D.C.: Brookings.

Patterson, Thomas, and Robert McClure (1976). *The Unseeing Eye: The Myth of Television Power in National Politics.* New York: Putnam.

Patterson, Thomas (1977). "Press Coverage and Candidate Success in Presidential Primaries: The 1976 Democratic Race." Paper delivered at the annual meeting of American Political Science Association.

Peirce, Neal (1968). *The People's President: The Electoral College in American History and the Direct-Vote Alternative*. New York: Simon & Schuster.

Polsby, Nelson, and Aaron Wildavsky (1964). *Presidential Elections: Strategies of American Electoral Politics*. New York: Scribner.

———— (1976). *Presidential Elections: Strategies of American Electoral Politics*, 4th ed. New York: Scribner.

Pomper, Gerald (1966). *Nominating the President: The Politics of Convention Choice*. New York: Norton.

———— (1975). *Voters' Choice: Varieties of American Electoral Behavior*. New York: Dodd Mead.

Pomper, Gerald (1977a). *The Election of 1976: Reports and Interpretations*. New York: David McKay.

Pomper, Gerald (1977b). "New Roles and New Games in the National Conventions." Paper delivered at the annual meeting of American Political Science Association.

Pressman, Jeffrey (1978). "Groups and Group Caucuses." *Political Science Quarterly, 92* (Winter): 673–682.

Ranney, Austin (1972). "Turnout and Representation in Presidential Primary Elections." *American Political Science Review, 66* (March): 21–37.

———— (1974). "Changing the Rules of the Nominating Game," in James David Barber (ed.), *Choosing the President*. Englewood Cliffs, N.J.: Prentice-Hall.

———— (1975). *Curing the Mischiefs of Faction: Party Reform in America*. Berkeley: University of California Press.

———— (1976). *Participation in American Presidential Nominations, 1976*. Washington, D.C.: American Enterprise Institute.

———— (1978a). *The Federalization of Presidential Primaries*. Washington, D.C.: American Enterprise Institute.

———— (1978b). "The Political Parties: Reform and Decline," in Anthony King (ed.), *The New American Political System*. Washington, D.C.: American Enterprise Institute.

Roche, John (1961). "The Founding Fathers: A Reform Caucus in Action." *American Political Science Review, 55* (December): 799–816.

Rubin, Richard (forthcoming). "Presidential Primaries: Continuities, Dimensions of Change, and Political Implications," in William Crotty (ed.), *The Party Symbol*, San Francisco, Cal.: Freeman.

Sayre, Wallace, and Judith Parris (1970). *Voting for President: The Electoral College and the American Political System*. Washington, D.C.: Brookings.

Schram, Martin (1977). *Running for President 1976: The Carter Campaign*. New York: Stein and Day.

Schumpeter, Joseph (1950). *Capitalism, Socialism and Democracy*, 3rd ed. New York: Harper & Row.

Stokes, Donald (1966). "Spatial Models of Party Completion," in Angus Campbell, Philip Converse, Warren Miller, and Donald Stokes, *Elections and the Political Order*. New York: Wiley.

Stroud, Kathy (1977). *How Jimmy Won: The Victory Campaign From Plains to the White House*. New York: William Morrow.

Sullivan, Denis, Jeffrey Pressman, and F. Christopher Arterton (1974). *Explorations in Convention Decision Making: The Democratic Party in the 1970's*. San Francisco: Freeman.

Weinberg, Martha (1978). "Writing the Republican Platform." *Political Science Quarterly,* *92* (Winter): 655–662.

White, Theodore (1961). *The Making of the President 1960.* New York: Pocket Books (Simon & Schuster).

——— (1965). *The Making of the President 1964.* New York: Signet (New American Library).

——— (1969). *The Making of the President 1968.* New York: Bantam.

——— (1973). *The Making of the President 1972.* New York: Bantam.

Wilmerding, Lucius (1958). *The Electoral College.* New Brunswick, N.J.: Rutgers University Press.

Witcover, Jules (1977). *Marathon: The Pursuit of the Presidency, 1972–1976.* New York: Viking.

Zeidenstein, Harvey (1970). "Presidential Primaries—Reflections of 'The People's Choice?'" *Journal of Politics, 32* (November): 856–874.

Guide to the 1980 Presidential Race

APPENDIX

Schedule of 1980 Presidential Primaries (Information as of August 1, 1979. Subject to change)

Date	State	Date	State
February 26	New Hampshire	May 6	Indiana
March 4	Massachusetts		North Carolina
	(April 15)*		Tennessee
	Vermont	May 13	Maryland
March 11	Alabama		Nebraska
	Florida	May 20	Michigan
March 16	Puerto Rico		Oregon
March 18	Illinois	May 27	Arkansas‡
March 25	Connecticut		Idaho
April 1	Kansas		Kentucky
	New York		Nevada
	(March 25 or	June 3	California
	April 29)*		Montana
	Wisconsin		New Jersey
April 5	Louisiana		New Mexico
April 22	Pennsylvania		Ohio
May 3	Texas† (March 11)*		Rhode Island
May 6	District of Columbia		South Dakota
	Georgia (March 11)*		West Virginia

*Possible alternative dates.
†Likely to be held only by Republicans.
‡For Democrats only.

B

Profiles of Major Candidates* for the 1980 Presidential Contest (Information available as of August 1, 1979. Subject to change)

DEMOCRATIC

1. *Edmund Brown, Jr.*—Lawyer. 41. Son of California Governor Edmund ("Pat") Brown, Sr., "Jerry" Brown graduated from Yale Law School. He was a member of the Los Angeles Crime Commission and served as secretary of state in California before becoming governor in 1975, a position he still holds. He was an unsuccessful Democratic presidential candidate in 1976 but, despite his late entry in the race, he defeated Jimmy Carter in the California, Maryland, and Nevada primaries. A fiscal conservative who has led a movement to amend the U.S. Constitution to restrict governmental expenditures, he is considered a liberal on environmental issues such as limiting the development of nuclear energy and has appointed blacks, Hispanics, and women to judicial positions in California.

2. *Jimmy Carter*—Farmer, engineer. 55. A graduate of the U.S. Naval Academy, the incumbent president began his career in civilian public life by serving as chairman of the school board in his hometown of Plains, Georgia. A moderate on the race issue who refused to join the White Citizens' Council, he served two terms in the state senate before making an unsuccessful gubernatorial attempt in 1966. He won the governorship in 1970 after a campaign in which he spoke out against federally imposed school desegregation plans and busing. Once in the office, how-

*Includes those who have formally announced their candidacy, established an official exploratory committee, or whose candidacy has been prominently mentioned in the national mass media.

ever, he hung Martin Luther King's portrait in the Statehouse and pursued a moderate course in race relations. In his one term in office (under Georgia state law he could not succeed himself), Carter reorganized the executive branch and reformed budgetary techniques in Georgia. He served as Democratic campaign coordinator for the 1974 midterm election and then began a concerted campaign that ultimately took him to the White House.

3. *Edward ("Ted") Kennedy*—Lawyer. 47. The younger brother of President John and Senator Robert Kennedy, Ted Kennedy graduated from the University of Virginia Law School and served one year as District Attorney of Suffolk County, Massachusetts, before being elected to the U.S. Senate at the age of 30. He served as Democratic whip from 1969 to 1971 before being ousted by the present Senate majority leader, Robert Byrd, and is presently the chairman of the Senate Judiciary Committee. Favored by many Democrats for their party's presidential nomination in 1972 and again in 1976, Kennedy refused to run. An exceptionally good public speaker with the reputation of having one of the ablest staffs in Washington, D.C., Senator Kennedy represents the liberal wing of the party and has taken the leadership on the issue of adequate health care for Americans through a compulsory insurance program. Kennedy's involvement in the accidental drowning of a young woman, Mary Jo Kopechne, at Chappaquiddick Island, Massachusetts in 1970, plus reported family problems, are considered by some persons to be major political liabilities for his presidential candidacy.

REPUBLICANS

1. *John Anderson*—Lawyer. 57. The recipient of law degrees from the University of Illinois and Harvard University, Anderson served as state's attorney of Winnebago County, Illinois prior to coming to the House of Representatives in 1961. Presently chairman of the House Republican Conference, he has a record of bipartisan voting in the Congress and is considered to be among the most liberal of the Republican presidential candidates. A target of "New Right" groups that tried unsuccessfully to defeat him in the 1978 congressional primary, he is expected to try to appeal to ethnic and minority groups. He is considered to be a "Son of the Midwest" and must do well in primaries and caucuses there if he is to become a major contender for the nomination.

2. *Howard Baker*—Lawyer. 54. The son-in-law of the late Senate Republican leader, Everett Dirksen, Baker received a law degree from the University of Tennessee and was a practicing attorney for seventeen years before coming to the Senate in 1967. Baker first came to national prominence during the Senate Watergate Committee hearings when he suggested that the committee focus its attention on "What the President knew and when he knew it." Elected Senate minority leader in 1977, Baker is considered a party centrist who has also played a key role in disputes over the Panama Canal and SALT II treaties.

3. *George Bush*—Businessman. 55. Son of former senator Prescott Bush of Connecticut, Bush received an undergraduate degree from Yale University and made a fortune as a drilling contractor in Texas. He was chairman of the Harris County Texas Republican Party and served as a U.S. Representative for four years. A loser in two Texas Senate races, he has held a number of high appointive positions, including ambassador to the United Nations, chairman of the Republican National Committee, chief of the U.S. Liason Office in Peking, and director of the Central Intelligence Agency. Considered a centrist, he has recruited a number of former aides of Gerald Ford, Ronald Reagan, and George Wallace to help with his campaign.

4. *John Connally*—Lawyer. 62. A graduate of the University of Texas Law School, Connally is a political protegé of former Democratic president Lyndon Johnson for whom Connally served as an administrative assistant when Johnson was a Senator from Texas. Secretary of the navy in the Kennedy administration, Connally was with the late president in Dallas and was wounded at the same time that Kennedy was assassinated. A member of the "regular" (conservative) faction of the Texas Democratic party, Connally was governor of Texas for six years. Subsequently he served as secretary of the treasury in the Nixon administration and later was adviser to the former president after Nixon got into the Watergate difficulties. Since breaking with the Democratic party, Connally has been active in Republican politics. Considered a political conservative who expresses his views in a forceful and articulate manner, his major political liability for the Republic nomination is his long association with the Democratic party; in addition, Connally was indicted (although later found innocent) of accepting an alleged bribe in connection with the raising of price supports for dairy products during the Nixon administration.

5. *Philip Crane*—Educator. 49. The recipient of a Ph.D from Indiana University and a former assistant professor of History at Bradley University, Crane has been a member of the Illinois delegation in the House of Representatives since 1969. A former supporter of Ronald Reagan (Crane is sometimes referred to as a "young" Ronald Reagan), he is probably the most conservative of the Republican candidates. Crane was a member of the "truth squad" of 20 congressmen who toured the country in 1978 in opposition to the ratification of the Panama Canal Treaty. He declared his candidacy in early August 1978—the first Republican to announce publicly for the presidency.

6. *Robert Dole*—Lawyer. 56. After receiving a law degree from Washburn University, Dole served in the Kansas state legislature and as prosecuting attorney of Russell County before coming to the House of Representatives in 1961 and then to the Senate in 1969. A former chairman of the Republican National Committee and the party's vice-presidential candidate in 1976, Dole has had a reputation of being a conservative and partisan fighter with a "hatchet man" image that he furthered during the 1976 campaign. However, since that time, he has tried to change that image, cosponsoring legislation with Democratic senator George McGovern to liberalize the food stamp program and promising in his presidential announcement statement not to attack President Carter or his Republican opponents in the 1980 campaign.

7. *Benjamin Fernandez*—Businessman, economist. 54. Born in a boxcar in Kansas City, Kansas, of Mexican immigrant parents, and the recipient of an undergraduate degree from the University of Redlands and a master's degree from New York University, Fernandez is a self-made Los Angeles millionaire. He first became active in politics in 1968 when he courted Spanish-American voters for the 1968 Nixon campaign. He was appointed to President Nixon's Council on Minority Business Enterprise and was chairman of the Hispanic Finance Committee to Reelect the President in 1972. He has also served on the executive committee of the Republican National Committee and is the founder and chairman of the Republican National Hispanic Assembly. An economic conservative who favors cutting the federal budget to counteract inflation and the deregulation of the oil and gas industry, he is more liberal on social issues, favoring a slowdown in the development of nuclear power and the outlawing of capital punishment. He also favors the development of closer ties with Latin American countries.

8. *Gerald Ford*—Lawyer. 66. A star football player at the University of Michigan, Ford received a law degree from Yale University and practiced law in his hometown of Grand Rapids, Michigan, before beginning his long career in the House of Representatives in 1949. A popular, hardworking member of the House with a conservative voting record, Ford got along well personally with members of varying political views from both political parties. He served as chairman of the House Republican Conference and as minority leader before being chosen as vice president by Richard Nixon following the resignation of Spiro Agnew. Ford succeeded to the presidency when Nixon resigned and, after defeating Ronald Reagan in a highly competitive nomination contest, went on to lose to Jimmy Carter in a close election in which Ford won more states (27) than Carter (23 plus the District of Columbia). Although Ford has said that he is not a candidate for the Republican nomination in 1980, he has indicated a willingness to accept it if no other candidate emerges as the clear favorite and the party turns to him as a compromise choice.

9. *Alexander Haig*—Soldier. 54. A career military officer for most of his life, Haig graduated from the U.S. Military Academy, the Army and Naval War Colleges, and also received a master's degree in International Relations from Georgetown University. He served in several executive positions relating to national security affairs prior to becoming chief of the White House staff following the resignation of H. R. Haldeman (who was implicated in the Watergate scandal). Haig is credited with influencing President Nixon to resign in August 1974 in order to avoid the trauma of the impeachment proceedings that would have been instituted against him. In 1974 Haig was appointed commander in chief of the U.S., European Command and commander of the North Atlantic Treaty Organization; he resigned from both those positions in 1979 and retired to civilian life.

10.   *Ronald Reagan*—Entertainer. 68. A graduate of Eureka College in Peoria, Illinois, Reagan was a well-known radio sports announcer in the Midwest before moving to California to begin a career first in movies and then in television. Initially he was a political liberal, active in The Screen Actors' Guild working for his fellow actors, but subsequently he became conservative and began making television appearances for General Electric. During the 1964 presidential campaign, Reagan gave the most effective speech for Goldwater and was encouraged two years later by wealthy businessmen to run for the governorship of California. Reagan served two terms in that position before beginning his unsuccessful bid in 1976 for the Republican nomination against the incumbent president, Gerald Ford. Traditionally considered to be very conservative, Reagan was responsible for the development of an innovative mental health program in California and demonstrated his willingness to broaden his political appeal by accepting a liberal Pennsylvania senator, Richard Schweiker, as his vice-presidential running mate in the 1976 nomination contest.

11.   *Harold Stassen*—Lawyer. 72. A perennial candidate for the Republican presidential nomination, Stassen received a law degree from the University of Minnesota and became governor of that state at the age of 31. He was the leading candidate for the presidential nomination in 1948 until he was defeated in a crucial primary in Oregon by the eventual Republican nominee, Thomas Dewey. He subsequently served as president of the University of Pennsylvania and as a special assistant for disarmament under President Eisenhower. Since that time he has practiced law in Philadelphia, Pennsylvania.

Rules for the 1980 Presidential Contest and 1976 Results—By State
(Information available as of August 1, 1979. Dates of Delegate Selection* and type of selection system† undetermined in some states. Also subject to change)

STATE: *ALABAMA*

Nomination

Date of Delegate
 Selection: *March 11*
Type of Selection
 System: *Primary*

*For caucus-conventions, the data indicated is for initial meetings held at the lowest political level.
†Those using any type of voting for presidential candidates are classified as primaries.

No. of Convention		
Votes:‡	Democratic: *45*	Republican: *27*
1976 Results (Number of		
Delegates)	Democratic:	Republican:
	Wallace—27	*Reagan—37 (All)*
	Uncommitted—5	

Election

No. of Electoral Votes:	*9*	
1976 Results (Percentage		
of Popular Votes)	Carter: *55.7*	Ford: *42.6*

STATE: *ALASKA*

Nomination

Date of Delegate		
Selection:	*Undetermined*	
Type of Selection		
System:	*Caucus-Convention*	
No. of Convention Votes:	Democratic: *11*	Republican: *19*
1976 Results (Number of		
Delegates)	Democratic:	Republican:
	Uncommitted—16	*Ford—17*
		Uncommitted—2

Election

No. of Electoral Votes:	*3*	
1976 Results (Percentage		
of Popular Votes)	Carter: *35.7*	Ford: *57.9*

STATE: *ARIZONA*

Nomination

Date of Delegate	
Selection:	*April 12 for Democrats;*
	Undetermined for
	Republicans
Type of Selection	
System:	*Caucus-Convention*

‡The total number of votes at the 1980 Democratic Convention will be 3331; the 1980 Republican National Convention will have at least 1993 and as many as 1996 votes if Republican governors are elected in 1979 in Kentucky, Louisiana, and Mississippi.

No. of Convention Votes:	Democratic: *29*	Republican: *28*
1976 Results (Number of		
Delegates)	Democratic:	Republican:
	Udall—19	*Reagan—27*
	Carter—5	*Ford—2*

Election

No. of Electoral Votes:	6	
1976 Results (Percentage		
of Popular Votes)	Carter: *39.8*	Ford: *56.4*

STATE: *ARKANSAS*

Nomination

Date of Delegate		
Selection:	*May 27*	
Type of Selection		
System:	*Primary for Democrats;*	
	Caucus-Convention for	
	Republicans	
No. of Convention Votes:	Democratic: *33*	Republican: *19*
1976 Results (*Percentage*		
of Votes)	Democratic:	Republican:
	Carter—62.6	*Reagan—63.4*
	Wallace—16.5	*Ford—35.1*

Election

No. of Electoral Votes:	6	
1976 Results (Percentage		
of Popular Votes)	Carter: *65.0*	Ford: *34.9*

STATE: *CALIFORNIA*

Nomination

Date of Delegate		
Selection:	*June 3*	
Type of Selection		
System:	*Primary*	
No. of Convention Votes:	Democratic: *306*	Republican: *168*
1976 Results (*Percentage*		
of Votes)	Democratic:	Republican:
	Brown—59.0	*Reagan—65.5*
	Carter—20.5	*Ford—34.5*

Election

No. of Electoral Votes:	*45*	
1976 Results (Percentage of Popular Votes)	Carter: *47.6*	Ford: *49.3*

STATE: *COLORADO*

Nomination

Date of Delegate Selection:	*May 5*	
Type of Selection System:	*Caucus-Convention*	
No. of Convention Votes:	Democratic: *40*	Republican: *31*
1976 Results (Number of Delegates)	Democratic: *Carter—12* *Uncommitted—9*	Republican: *Reagan—26* *Ford—4*

Election

No. of Electoral Votes:	*7*	
1976 Results (Percentage of Popular Votes)	Carter: *42.6*	Ford: *54.0*

STATE: *CONNECTICUT*

Nomination

Date of Delegate Selection:	*March 25*	
Type of Selection System:	*Primary*	
No. of Convention Votes:	Democratic: *54*	Republican: *35*
1976 Results	Democratic: (*Percentage of Votes*) *Carter—33.2* *Udall—30.8*	Republican: (*Number of Delegates*) *Ford—35 (All)*

Election

No. of Electoral Votes:	*8*	
1976 Results (Percentage of Popular Votes)	Carter: *46.9*	Ford: *52.1*

STATE: *DELAWARE*

Nomination

Date of Delegate Selection:	*Between March 17–April 5 for Democrats; Undetermined for Republicans*	
Type of Selection System:	*Caucus-Convention*	
No. of Convention Votes:	Democratic: *14*	Republican: *12*
1976 Results (*Number of Delegates*)	Democratic: Carter—*10* Uncommitted—*2*	Republican: Ford—*13* Uncommitted—*4*

Election

No. of Electoral Votes:	*3*	
1976 Results (Percentage of Popular Votes)	Carter: *52.0*	Ford: *46.6*

STATE: *FLORIDA*

Nomination

Date of Delegate Selection:	*March 11*	
Type of Selection System:	*Primary*	
No. of Convention Votes:	Democratic: *100*	Republican: *51*
1976 Results (*Percentage of Votes*)	Democratic: Carter—*34.5* Wallace—*30.5*	Republican: Ford—*52.8* Reagan—*47.2*

Election

No. of Electoral Votes:	*17*	
1976 Results (Percentage of Popular Votes)	Carter: *51.9*	Ford: *46.6*

STATE: *GEORGIA*

Nomination

Date of Delegate Selection:	May 6 or March 11	
Type of Selection System:	*Primary*	
No. of Convention Votes:	Democratic: *63*	Republican: *36*
1976 Results (*Percentage of Votes*)	Democratic: *Carter—83.4* *Wallace—11.5*	Republican: *Reagan—68.3* *Ford—31.7*

Election

No. of Electoral Votes:	*12*	
1976 Results (Percentage of Popular Votes)	Carter: *66.7*	Ford: *33.0*

STATE: *HAWAII*

Nomination

Date of Delegate Selection:	*March 11 for Democrats;* *Undetermined for* *Republicans*	
Type of Selection System:	*Caucus-Convention*	
No. of Convention Votes:	Democratic: *19*	Republican: *14*
1976 Results (*Number of Delegates*)	Democratic: *Uncommitted—15* *Jackson—1* *Udall—1*	Republican: *Ford—15* *Uncommitted—3*

Election

No. of Electoral Votes:	*4*	
1976 Results (Percentage of Popular Votes)	Carter: *50.6*	Ford: *48.1*

STATE: *IDAHO*

Nomination

Date of Delegate Selection:	*May 27*	
Type of Selection System:	*Primary*	
No. of Convention Votes:	Democratic: *17*	Republican: *21*
1976 Results (*Percentage of Votes*)	Democratic: *Church—78.7* *Carter—11.9*	Republican: *Reagan—74.3* *Ford—24.9*

Election

No. of Electoral Votes:	*4*	
1976 Results (Percentage of Popular Votes)	Carter: *36.8*	Ford: *59.3*

STATE: *ILLINOIS*

Nomination

Date of Delegate Selection:	*March 18*	
Type of Selection System:	*Primary*	
No. of Convention Votes:	Democratic: *179*	Republican: *102*
1976 Results (*Percentage of Votes*)	Democratic: *Carter—48.1* *Wallace—27.6*	Republican: *Ford—58.9* *Reagan—40.1*

Election

No. of Electoral Votes:	*26*	
1976 Results (Percentage of Popular Votes)	Carter: *48.1*	Ford: *50.1*

STATE: *INDIANA*

Nomination

Date of Delegate Selection:	*May 6*
Type of Selection System:	*Primary*

No. of Convention Votes: Democratic: *80*   Republican: *54*
1976 Results (*Percentage*
   of Votes)   Democratic: Republican
                      Carter—68.0   *Reagan—51.3*
                      Wallace—15.2   *Ford—48.7*

Election

No. of Electoral Votes: *13*
1976 Results (Percentage
   of Popular Votes)   Carter: *45.7*   Ford: *53.3*

STATE: *IOWA*

Date of Delegate
   Selection: *January 21*
Type of Selection
   System: *Caucus-Convention*
No. of Convention Votes: Democratic: *50*   Republican: *37*
1976 Results (*Number of*
   Delegates)   Democratic: Republican:
                      Carter—20   *Ford—19*
                      Udall—12   *Reagan—17*

Election

No. of Electoral Votes: *8*
1976 Results (Percentage
   of Popular Votes)   Carter: *48.5*   Ford: *49.5*

STATE: *KANSAS*

Nomination

Date of Delegate
   Selection: *April 1*
Type of Selection
   System: *Primary*
No. of Convention Votes: Democratic: *37*   Republican: *32*
1976 Results (*Number of*
   Delegates)   Democratic: Republican:
                      Carter—16   *Ford—29*
                      Uncommitted—14   *Reagan—4*

Election

No. of Electoral Votes: *7*
1976 Results (Percentage
   of Popular Votes)   Carter: *44.9*   Ford: *52.5*

STATE: *KENTUCKY*

Nomination

Date of Delegate Selection:	*May 27*	
Type of Selection System:	*Primary*	
No. of Convention Votes:	Democratic: *50*	Republican: *27 or 28*

1976 Results (*Percentage of Votes*)	Democratic:
	    Carter—59.4
	    Wallace—16.8
		Republican:
		    Ford—50.9
		    Reagan—46.9

Election

No. of Electoral Votes:	*9*	
1976 Results (Percentage of Popular Votes)	Carter: *52.8*	Ford: *45.6*

STATE: *LOUISIANA*

Nomination

Date of Delegate Selection:	*April 5*	
Type of Selection System:	*Primary*	
No. of Convention Votes:	Democratic: *51*	Republican: *30 or 31*

1976 Results (*Number of Delegates*)	Democratic:
	    Uncommitted—19
	    Carter—13
		Republican:
		    Reagan—36
		    Uncommitted—5

Election

No. of Electoral Votes:	*10*	
1976 Results (Percentage of Popular Votes)	Carter: *57.7*	Ford: *46.0*

STATE: *MAINE*

Nomination

Date of Delegate Selection:	*February 10 for Democrats; Sometime in February for Republicans*

Type of Selection System:	*Caucus-Convention*	
No. of Convention Votes:	Democratic: *22*	Republican: *21*
1976 Results (*Number of Delegates*)	Democratic:	Republican:
	Carter—9	*Ford—15*
	Udall—5	*Reagan—4*

Election

No. of Electoral Votes:	*4*	
1976 Results (Percentage of Popular Votes)	Carter: *48.1*	Ford: *48.9*

STATE: *MARYLAND*

Nomination

Date of Delegate Selection:	*May 13*	
Type of Selection System:	*Primary*	
No. of Convention Votes:	Democratic: *59*	Republican: *30*
1976 Results (*Percentage of Votes*)	Democratic:	Republican:
	Brown—48.4	*Ford—58.0*
	Carter—37.1	*Reagan—42.0*

Election

No. of Electoral Votes:	*10*	
1976 Results (Percentage of Popular Votes)	Carter: *52.8*	Ford: *46.7*

STATE: *MASSACHUSETTS*

Nomination

Date of Delegate Selection:	*March 4 or April 15*	
Type of Selection System:	*Primary*	
No. of Convention Votes:	Democratic: *111*	Republican: *42*
1976 Results (*Percentage of Votes*)	Democratic:	Republican:
	Jackson—22.3	*Ford—61.2*
	Udall—17.7	*Reagan—33.7*

Election

No. of Electoral Votes:	*14*	
1976 Results (Percentage of Popular Votes)	Carter: *56.1*	Ford: *40.4*

STATE: *MICHIGAN*

Nomination

Date of Delegate Selection:	*May 20*	
Type of Selection System:	*Primary*	
No. of Convention Votes:	Democratic: *141*	Republican: *82*

1976 Results (*Percentage of Votes*)	Democratic:
	  Carter—43.4
	  Udall—43.1
		Republican:
		  Ford—64.9
		  Reagan—34.3

Election

No. of Electoral Votes:	*21*	
1976 Results (Percentage of Popular Votes)	Carter: *46.4*	Ford: *51.8*

STATE: *MINNESOTA*

Nomination

Date of Delegate Selection:	*February 26*	
Type of Selection System:	*Caucus-Convention*	
No. of Convention Votes:	Democratic: *75*	Republican: *34*

1976 Results (*Number of Delegates*)	Democratic:
	  Humphrey—48
	  Uncommitted—17
		Republican
		  Ford—32
		  Reagan—6

Election

No. of Electoral Votes:	*10*	
1976 Results (Percentage of Popular Votes)	Carter: *54.9*	Ford: *42.0*

STATE: *MISSISSIPPI*

Nomination

Date of Delegate
  Selection:

January 26 for Democrats; Sometime in March for Republicans

Type of Selection
  System:

Caucus-Convention for Democrats; Republicans may use a Primary

No. of Convention Votes: Democratic: *32*   Republican: *22 or 23*
1976 Results (*Number of*
  Delegates)

Democratic: Republican:
  Wallace—11   *Uncommitted—30 (All)*
  Carter—5

Election

No. of Electoral Votes: *7*
1976 Results (Percentage
  of Popular Votes)   Carter: *49.6*   Ford: *47.7*

STATE: *MISSOURI*

Nomination

Date of Delegate
  Selection:

April 22 for Democrats; Sometime in June for Republicans

Type of Selection
  System: *Caucus-Convention*
No. of Convention Votes: Democratic: *77*   Republican: *37*
1976 Results (*Number of*
  Delegates)

Democratic: Republican:
  Carter—39   *Reagan—30*
  Uncommitted—27   *Ford—16*

Election

No. of Electoral Votes: *12*
1976 Results (Percentage
  of Popular Votes)   Carter: *51.1*   Ford: *47.5*

STATE: *MONTANA*

Nomination

Date of Delegate Selection:	*June 3*	
Type of Selection System:	*Primary*	
No. of Convention Votes:	Democratic: *19*	Republican: *20*
1976 Results (*Percentage of Votes*)	Democratic: *Church—59.4* *Carter—24.6*	Republican: *Reagan—63.1* *Ford—34.6*

Election

No. of Electoral Votes:	*4*	
1976 Results (Percentage of Popular Votes)	Carter: *45.4*	Ford: *52.8*

STATE: *NEBRASKA*

Nomination

Date of Delegate Selection:	*May 13*	
Type of Selection System:	*Primary*	
No. of Convention Votes:	Democratic: *24*	Republican: *25*
1976 Results (*Percentage of Votes*)	Democratic: *Church—38.5* *Carter—37.6*	Republican: *Reagan—54.5* *Ford—45.4*

Election

No. of Electoral Votes:	*5*	
1976 Results (Percentage of Popular Votes)	Carter: *38.5*	Ford: *59.2*

STATE: *NEVADA*

Nomination

Date of Delegate Selection:	*May 27*
Type of Selection System:	*Primary*

No. of Convention Votes: Democratic: *12* Republican: *17*
1976 Results (*Percentage
of Votes*) Democratic: Republican:
  Brown—52.7 *Reagan—66.3*
  Carter—23.3 *Ford—28.8*

Election

No. of Electoral Votes: *3*
1976 Results (Percentage
of Popular Votes) Carter: *45.8* Ford: *50.2*

STATE: *NEW HAMPSHIRE*

Nomination

Date of Delegate
  Selection: *February 26*
Type of Selection
  System: *Primary*
No. of Convention Votes: Democratic: *19* Republican: *22*
1976 Results (*Percentage
of Votes*) Democratic: Republican:
  Carter—28.4 *Ford—49.4*
  Udall—22.7 *Reagan—48.0*

Election

No. of Electoral Votes: *4*
1976 Results (Percentage
of Popular Votes) Carter: *43.5* Ford: *54.7*

STATE: *NEW JERSEY*

Nomination

Date of Delegate
  Selection: *June 3*
Type of Selection
  System: *Primary*
No. of Convention Votes: Democratic: *113* Republican: *66*
1976 Results (*Percentage
of Votes*) Democratic: Republican:
  Carter—58.4 *Ford—100.0*
  Church—13.6

Election

No. of Electoral Votes:	*7*	
1976 Results (Percentage of Popular Votes)	Carter: *47.9*	Ford: *50.1*

STATE: *NEW MEXICO*

Nomination

Date of Delegate Selection:	*June 3*	
Type of Selection System:	*Primary*	
No. of Convention Votes:	Democratic: *20*	Republican: *22*
1976 Results (*Number of Delegates*)	Democratic: Carter—8 Udall—6	Republican: Reagan—21 (All)

Election

No. of Electoral Votes:	*4*	
1976 Results (Percentage of Popular Votes)	Carter: *48.1*	Ford: *50.5*

STATE: *NEW YORK*

Nomination

Date of Delegate Selection:	*April 1, March 25, or April 29*	
Type of Selection System:	*Primary*	
No. of Convention Votes:	Democratic: *282*	Republican: *123*
1976 Results (*Number of Delegates*)	Democratic: Jackson—103 Udall—73	Republican: Uncommitted—154 (All)

Election

No. of Electoral Votes:	*41*	
1976 Results (Percentage of Popular Votes)	Carter: *51.9*	Ford: *47.5*

STATE: *NORTH CAROLINA*

Nomination

Date of Delegate Selection:	*May 6*	
Type of Selection System:	*Primary*	
No. of Convention Votes:	Democratic: *69*	Republican: *40*
1976 Results (*Percentage of Votes*)	Democratic: *Carter—53.6* *Wallace—34.7*	Republican: *Reagan—52.4* *Ford—45.9*

Election

No. of Electoral Votes:	*13*	
1976 Results (Percentage of Popular Votes)	Carter: *55.2*	Ford: *44.2*

STATE: *NORTH DAKOTA*

Nomination

Date of Delegate Selection:	*Undetermined*	
Type of Selection System:	*Caucus-Convention*	
No. of Convention Votes:	Democratic: *14*	Republican: *17*
1976 Results (*Number of Delegates*)	Democratic: *Carter—13 (All)*	Republican: *Ford—11* *Reagan—5*

Election

No. of Electoral Votes:	*3*	
1976 Results (Percentage of Popular Votes)	Carter: *45.8*	Ford: *51.6*

STATE: *OHIO*

Nomination

Date of Delegate Selection:	*June 3*
Type of Selection System:	*Primary*

No. of Convention Votes:	Democratic: *161*	Republican: *77*
1976 Results (*Percentage*		
of Votes)	Democratic:	Republican:
	Carter—52.3	*Ford—55.2*
	Udall—21.0	*Reagan—44.8*

Election

No. of Electoral Votes:	*25*	
1976 Results (Percentage		
of Popular Votes)	Carter: *48.9*	Ford: *48.7*

STATE: *OKLAHOMA*

Nomination

Date of Delegate		
Selection:	*March 11*	
Type of Selection		
System:	*Caucus-Convention*	
No. of Convention Votes:	Democratic: *42*	Republican: *34*
1976 Results (*Number of*		
Delegates)	Democratic:	Republican:
	Uncommitted—18	*Reagan—36 (All)*
	Carter—12	

Election

No. of Electoral Votes:	*8*	
1976 Results (Percentage		
of Popular Votes)	Carter: *48.7*	Ford: *50.0*

STATE: *OREGON*

Nomination

Date of Delegate		
Selection:	*May 20*	
Type of Selection		
System:	*Primary*	
No. of Convention Votes:	Democratic: *39*	Republican: *29*
1976 Results (*Percentage*		
of Votes)	Democratic:	Republican:
	Church—33.6	*Ford—50.3*
	Carter—26.7	*Reagan—45.8*

Election

No. of Electoral Votes: 6
1976 Results (Percentage
  of Popular Votes)   Carter: *47.6*   Ford: *47.8*

STATE: *PENNSYLVANIA*

Nomination

Date of Delegate
  Selection: *April 22*
Type of Selection
  System: *Primary*
No. of Convention Votes: Democratic: *185*   Republican: *83*
1976 Results (*Percentage
  of Votes*)   Democratic: Republican:
                              Carter—37.0   *Ford—92.1*
                              Jackson—24.6   *Reagan—5.1*

Election

No. of Electoral Votes: 27
1976 Results (Percentage
  of Popular Votes)   Carter: *50.4*   Ford: *47.7*

STATE: *RHODE ISLAND*

Nomination

Date of Delegate
  Selection: *June 3*
Type of Selection
  System: *Primary*
No. of Convention Votes: Democratic: *23*   Republican: *13*
1976 Results (*Percentage
  of Votes*)   Democratic: Republican:
                              Uncommitted—31.5   *Ford—65.3*
                              Carter—30.2   *Reagan—31.2*

Election

No. of Electoral Votes: 4
1976 Results (Percentage
  of Popular Votes)   Carter: *55.4*   Ford: *44.1*

STATE: *SOUTH CAROLINA*

Nomination

Date of Delegate Selection:	*March 15 for Democrats; Undetermined for Republicans*	
Type of Selection System:	*Caucus-Convention for Democrats; Republicans may use a Primary*	
No. of Convention Votes:	Democratic: *37*	Republican: *25*
1976 Results (*Number of Delegates*)	Democratic: *Uncommitted—13 Carter—9*	Republican: *Reagan—26 Ford—7*

Election

No. of Electoral Votes:	*8*	
1976 Results (Percentage of Popular Votes)	Carter: *56.2*	Ford: *43.1*

STATE: *SOUTH DAKOTA*

Nomination

Date of Delegate Selection:	*June 3*	
Type of Selection System:	*Primary*	
No. of Convention Votes:	Democratic: *19*	Republican: *22*
1976 Results (*Percentage of Votes*)	Democratic: *Carter—41.2 Udall—33.3*	Republican: *Reagan—51.2 Ford—44.0*

Election

No. of Electoral Votes:	*4*	
1976 Results (Percentage of Popular Votes)	Carter: *48.9*	Ford: *50.4*

STATE: *TENNESSEE*

Nomination

Date of Delegate
  Selection: *May 6*
Type of Selection
  System: *Primary*
No. of Convention Votes: Democratic: *55*   Republican: *32*
1976 Results (*Percentage
  of Votes*)   Democratic: Republican:
         Carter—77.6   *Ford—49.8*
         Wallace—10.9   *Reagan—49.1*

Election

No. of Electoral Votes: *10*
1976 Results (Percentage
  of Popular Votes)   Carter: *55.9*   Ford: *42.9*

STATE: *TEXAS*

Nomination

Date of Delegate
  Selection: *May 3 or March 11*
Type of Selection
  System: *Probably
       Caucus-Convention for
       Democrats and
       Primary for
       Republicans*
No. of Convention Votes: Democratic: *152*   Republican: *80*
1976 Results (*Number of
  Delegates*)   Democratic: Republican:
         Carter—112   *Reagan—100 (All)*
         Uncommitted—9

Election

No. of Electoral Votes: *26*
1976 Results (Percentage
  of Popular Votes)   Carter: *51.1*   Ford: *48.0*

STATE: *UTAH*

Nomination

Date of Delegate Selection:	*May 19 for Democrats; Undetermined for Republicans*	
Type of Selection System:	*Caucus-Convention*	
No. of Convention Votes:	Democratic: *20*	Republican: *21*
1976 Results (*Number of Delegates*)	Democratic: *Uncommitted—9* *Church—5*	Republican: *Reagan—20 (All)*

Election

No. of Electoral Votes:	*4*	
1976 Results (Percentage of Popular Votes)	Carter: *33.6*	Ford: *62.4*

STATE: *VERMONT*

Nomination

Date of Delegate Selection:	*March 4*	
Type of Selection System:	*Primary*	
No. of Convention Votes:	Democratic: *12*	Republican: *19*
1976 Results (*Percentage of Votes*)	Democratic: *Carter—42.2* *Shriver—27.6*	Republican: *Ford—84.0* *Reagan—15.2*

Election

No. of Electoral Votes:	*3*	
1976 Results (Percentage of Popular Votes)	Carter: *43.1*	Ford: *54.4*

STATE: *VIRGINIA*

Nomination

Date of Delegate
  Selection: *March 15 for Democrats;*
                            Undetermined for
                            Republicans

Type of Selection
  System: *Caucus-Convention*
No. of Convention Votes: Democratic: *64*   Republican: *51*
1976 Results (*Number of*
  Delegates)   Democratic: Republican:
                              Uncommitted—24   *Reagan—35*
                              Carter—23   *Uncommitted—10*

Election

No. of Electoral Votes: *12*
1976 Results (Percentage
  of Popular Votes)   Carter: *48.0*   Ford: *49.3*

STATE: *WASHINGTON*

Nomination

Date of Delegate
  Selection: *March 11 for Democrats;*
                            Undetermined for
                            Republicans

Type of Selection
  System: *Caucus-Convention*
No. of Convention Votes: Democratic: *58*   Republican: *37*
1976 Results (*Number of*
  Delegates)   Democratic: Republican:
                              Jackson—32   *Reagan—31*
                              Uncommitted—14   *Ford—7*

Election

No. of Electoral Votes: *9*
1976 Results (Percentage
  of Popular Votes)   Carter: *46.1*   Ford: *50.0*

STATE: *WEST VIRGINIA*

Nomination

Date of Delegate Selection:	*June 3*	
Type of Selection System:	*Primary*	
No. of Convention Votes:	Democratic: *35*	Republican: *18*
1976 Results (*Percentage of Votes*)	Democratic: Byrd—89.0 Wallace—11.0	Republican: Ford—56.8 Reagan—43.2

Election

No. of Electoral Votes:	6	
1976 Results (Percentage of Popular Votes)	Carter: *58.0*	Ford: *41.9*

STATE: *WISCONSIN*

Nomination

Date of Delegate Selection:	*April 1*	
Type of Selection System:	*Primary*	
No. of Convention Votes:	Democratic: *75*	Republican: *34*
1976 Results (*Percentage of Votes*)	Democratic: Carter—36.6 Udall—35.6	Republican: Ford—55.2 Reagan—44.3

Election

No. of Electoral Votes:	*11*	
1976 Results (Percentage of Popular Votes)	Carter: *49.4*	Ford: *47.8*

STATE: *WYOMING*

Nomination

Date of Delegate Selection:	*March 1–15 for Democrats; Sometime in March for Republicans*

Type of Selection
 System: *Caucus-Convention*
No. of Convention Votes: Democratic: *11*   Republican: *19*
1976 Results (*Number of*
 Delegates)   Democratic: Republican:
                                   Uncommitted—7   *Uncommitted—17 (All)*
                                   Brown—1
                                   Carter—1
                                   Udall—1

Election

No. of Electoral Votes: *3*
1976 Results (Percentage
 of Popular Votes)   Carter: *39.8*   Ford: *59.3*

DISTRICT OF COLUMBIA

Nomination

Date of Delegate
 Selection: *May 6*
Type of Selection
 System: *Primary*
No. of Convention Votes: Democratic: *19*   Republican: *14*
1976 Results (*Percentage*
 of Votes)   Democratic: Republican:
                                   Carter—31.6   *Ford unopposed, no*
                                                                       primary held
                                   Fauntroy—30.5

Election

No. of Electoral Votes: *3*
1976 Results (Percentage
 of Popular Votes)   Carter: *81.6*   Ford: *16.5*

Index